Equipping Young People to Choose Non-Violence

of related interest

From Violence to Resilience
Positive Transformative Programmes to Grow Young Leaders
Jo Broadwood and Nic Fine
ISBN 978 1 84905 183 5

Playing with Fire
Training for Those Working with Young People in Conflict
2nd edition
Fiona Macbeth and Nic Fine
With Jo Broadwood, Carey Haslam and Nik Pitcher
ISBN 978 1 84905 184 2

How to Be Angry
An Assertive Anger Expression Group Guide for Kids and Teens
Signe Whitson
Foreword by Dr Nicholas Long
ISBN 978 1 84905 867 4

What Have I Done?
A Victim Empathy Programme for Young People
Pete Wallis
With Clair Aldington and Marian Liebmann
ISBN 978 1 84310 979 2

Working with Gangs and Young People
A Toolkit for Resolving Group Conflict
Jessie Feinstein and Nia Imani Kuumba
ISBN 978 1 84310 447 6

The Pocket Guide to Restorative Justice
Pete Wallis and Barbara Tudor
ISBN 978 1 84310 629 6

Just Schools
A Whole School Approach to Restorative Justice
Belinda Hopkins
ISBN 978 1 84310 132 1

Just Care
Restorative Justice Approaches to Working with Children in Public Care
Belinda Hopkins
Foreword by Jonathan Stanley
ISBN 978 1 84310 981 5

Equipping Young People to Choose Non-Violence

A Violence Reduction Programme to Understand Violence, Its Effects, Where It Comes From and How to Prevent It

GERRY HEERY

Jessica Kingsley *Publishers*
London and Philadelphia

First published in 2012
by Jessica Kingsley Publishers
116 Pentonville Road
London N1 9JB, UK
and
400 Market Street, Suite 400
Philadelphia, PA 19106, USA

www.jkp.com

Library of Congress Cataloging in Publication Data
Heery, Gerry.
  Equipping young people to choose non-violence : a violence reduction programme to understand violence, its effects, where it comes from and how to prevent it / Gerry Heery.
    p. cm.
  ISBN 978-1-84905-265-8 (alk. paper)
 1. Youth and violence--Prevention. 2. Youth and violence. 3. Nonviolence.
I. Title.
  HQ799.2.V56H44 2012
  303.6'90835--dc23
                            2011016824

British Library Cataloguing in Publication Data
A CIP catalogue record for this book is available from the British Library

ISBN 978 1 84905 265 8
eISBN 978 0 85700 605 9

Printed and bound in Great Britain

In memory of my father, William Heery, and to my mother-in-law, Grace Hasson, both of whom, in their own ways, helped me to choose non-violence.

Contents

List of Handouts

Acknowledgements

This publication reflects my experiences of working with many young people, their families and communities over the past 25 years in Northern Ireland. I have been privileged to work with many committed colleagues within statutory family and childcare, youth justice and probation services, and associated voluntary and community sectors. It is from these that I have received much guidance, encouragement and support, particularly in seeking to respond to many and varied situations of violence.

I am particularly indebted to Alice Chapman OBE and Kelvin Doherty from the Youth Justice Agency in Northern Ireland who offered me the opportunity to tailor my experience to draw up a programme aimed specifically at young people experiencing and presenting difficulties in their lives through the use of violence.

Thanks also to Greg Walker, Laura Brownlow, Linda Humphrey and Alan Harris from the same agency who facilitated the pilot of this programme during the autumn and winter of 2009/10 and were able to provide helpful feedback on the manual design and content.

The young people who participated in these sessions have also provided me with useful comment and feedback.

Of course, none of the above are responsible for any errors or shortcomings in the Choosing Non-Violence programme.

Introduction

'…the last of the human freedoms – To choose one's attitude in any given set of circumstances, to choose one's own way.'

Viktor Frankl (2004, p.75)

Violence and its use by young people – within family relationships, among their network of friends and acquaintances, within their communities, and against members of particular groups or other communities, has played a significant role in my professional life. Within days of beginning my career as a trainee social worker in a large residential centre for young people in Northern Ireland, I encountered two young people facing each other clearly in some sort of conflict.

Suddenly and without warning, one of the young men head-butted the other in the face and continued lashing out with his fists and feet as his 'victim' fell to the ground before I and another member of staff could pull him off. At the time, I was convinced that the young man was the aggressor and his behaviour totally unacceptable. It was only in later discussing the incident further with the two young people involved and other bystanders that I became aware of a different view. The young person who had been struck had made an almost imperceptible movement with his hand – taking it out of one of his pockets – which justified the attack by the other. Both parties and the other young men who were watching all took this view!

Over 25 years later, I was working with a father, deeply concerned about his teenage daughter who was being bullied at school. He had gone to the school to try to get the matter sorted out but with little success. In desperation, after his daughter had once again come home in a distressed state, he told her that the next time she was bullied to 'fucking punch the bitch and let her know that she wasn't going to take any more shit from her'.

The above examples are just two of the many encounters I have had with young people using violence in their lives; every incident different in its own way, some more traumatic than others. However, the examples bear witness to the idea that violence is really the only way to handle situations of conflict or tension. Indeed, it is an unavoidable strategy that many young people need to help them cope with their lives.

The Choosing Non-Violence programme, in a sense, represents my response to such a view. It rests on the belief that violence is not natural and part of the human condition. Neither is it something mysterious which just happens, nor is it always the result of anger and blind rage. The programme begins by recognizing the complexity of violence; nevertheless, it is offered as an educational and preventative resource that can engage with young people in a meaningful and purposeful way about the use of violence in their lives and give a vision that there are other ways. As Viktor Frankl pointed out many years ago, when experiencing the unspeakable violence of a concentration camp, there is always the power to choose.

The programme consists of 12 individual sessions grounded in a restorative ethos to challenge the young person to explore and address his or her use of violence. It is an individually delivered one-to-one programme in which the young person will be encouraged and supported to take responsibility for the use of violence; recognize the hurt it causes; identify possible ways to repair the harm; and learn new skills to help in avoiding future violence. It is intended as a resource for anyone working with young people – social worker, teacher, youth worker, youth justice worker, mental health worker or counsellor – and where the issue of violent and aggressive behaviour by the young person is giving rise to concerns.

The starting point with any endeavour in life is to be clear about the principles, knowledge and values that give it drive and direction. Part 1, therefore, commences with a chapter on the foundation of the Choosing Non-Violence programme, the value and evidence base upon which it rests, and the elements required to carry out the work in an effective and ethical way. It seeks to explain the theoretical underpinnings in a way that makes complex material accessible to busy and hard-pressed workers – to make things simple but not simplistic – and to give clear guidance on the approach required from those delivering the programme.

Chapter 2 goes on to outline the basic structure of the programme and how a facilitator should approach running it.

Finally, Chapter 3 explores how the programme can be evaluated, examining the needs of anyone who may wish to use all or part of this programme to reflect on their practice and to seek to ensure that what they do is both ethical and effective. To this end, quality assurance, monitoring and evaluation issues are considered. It also outlines measures that agencies should consider taking if they intend to adapt and use the programme in its entirety as one of their services. It is important to build in various support and monitoring systems to ensure programme integrity and a positive service to each young person.

Part 2 forms the heart of the resource, outlining the structure and make-up of each of the 12 sessions.

Appendix 1 contains a selection of exercises for use within the final element of each session, while Appendix 2 includes evaluation forms – the usefulness of which is explained in Chapter 3.

Part I
Background

Chapter 1
Foundations of the Choosing Non-Violence Programme

'I am capable of what every other human being is capable of. This is one of the great lessons of war and life.'

Maya Angelou

I wrote down the words of Maya Angelo, which I heard on a long-forgotten television programme, and they have stayed with me. They challenge me, and anyone wishing to help another person deal with their use of violence, to recognize that it is something that everyone is capable of using. The Choosing Non-Violence programme will provide a creative, constructive and challenging learning experience for the young person to address his or her use of violence in a restorative and pro-social way.

Each young person will be encouraged to take responsibility for their behaviour; to gain a greater understanding of why it is happening; to appreciate more profoundly the effects it may have on others and themselves; to find ways to address the harm caused by their behaviour; to develop skills to handle conflict without the use of violence, and ultimately to commit themselves to choosing non-violent future behaviours.

To this end, it provides a structured intervention, with pre-set aims, measurable objectives and relevant content. The challenge is to pull together a wide range of theoretical material and present it in ways that meet the needs and learning styles of individual young people and to provide a challenging opportunity to do necessary personal work.

The ethical practice base: Values

The Choosing Non-Violence programme is aligned with a restorative ethos. The key values upon which the programme rests, and which will require the commitment of those who choose to facilitate it, are respect for the young person; promotion of his or her self-determination; promotion of social justice;

and working for his or her interests (and also for the interests of those who have been the victims of the young person's violence). These are congruent with the values underpinning education, social work, youth work and counselling approaches in many countries of the world (Banks 2006).

This means that the young person is viewed as a human being, not a problem to be solved. Each young person will be seen as an individual with a dignity beyond measure, and a personal core that is unique to that young person, with his or her own viewpoint and learning style. The programme will recognize and support the developmental needs of each young person. It will also actively encourage the individual young person to become more aware of their needs and involve them in planning and decision-making as to how best to deal with their use of violence in ways that recognize and take account of the harm caused to others.

The creativity of each young person in carrying this out will be valued and encouraged through a positive process of learning and discovery. The programme's recognition of the young person's experience and the involvement of some young people in contributing to the piloting and design of this programme reflects this value base.

The ethical practice base: Knowledge

Ethical practice also demands that the programme is founded on reliable knowledge. In this regard, the programme design seeks to reflect current literature and research, which is continually emerging, and aims to make it accessible to practitioners in ways that allow them continuously to improve and develop practice. This involves gathering a wide variety of diverse but relevant material and trying to reassemble it in a useful and creative way. It is about trying to help practitioners deliver this material in down-to-earth language that can connect to the young people. Critically, the facilitator needs to avoid the use of jargon that can have the effect of creating unnecessary barriers by reinforcing power differences and also of alienating young people (Thompson 2003).

The application of theory is not straightforward for various reasons. Primarily, in dealing with human behaviour the science can be inconsistent, contested and difficult to apply. This is particularly the case in seeking to devise a programme addressing violent behaviour. Violence is an enormously complex, multi-determined range of behaviours (Gilligan 2000). As one eminent researcher in the field has stated, 'There are far more statistics about violence than there is knowledge' (Stanko 2002, p.42). The bottom line remains that there is no universal agreement as to what actually defines violence and why some people are violent.

For the purposes of this programme, violence will be defined as the intentional use of physical force or power, threatened or actual, used by the young person against another person, group or community that results in, or has a high likelihood of resulting in, injury, psychological harm, mal-development or deprivation (WHO 2004). In terms of explaining involvement in such behaviour, the programme design will reflect the view that no single factor explains why one person and not another behaves in a violent manner. It is better to work with a set of alternative interpretive frameworks rather than a single-minded assumption that every case of violence fits the same pattern.

The ecological model

The World Health Organization has promoted the notion of seeing violence within societies as a public health issue (WHO 2004). Violence is viewed as a complex problem rooted in the interaction of many factors – biological, social, cultural, economic and political. It is important that this complexity is recognized and a certain degree of realism and humility is in place in seeking to meet the challenge of basing the programme on a reasonable body of evidence.

It needs to be grounded in the research that indicates what is likely to be most helpful to young people in encouraging them to move away from the use of violence in their lives. To this end, the World Health Organization's report on violence and health (WHO 2002) uses an ecological model to try to understand the multifaceted nature of violence. First introduced in the late 1970s for the study of child abuse and subsequently used in other fields of violence research, the ecological model is still being developed and refined as a conceptual tool (WHO 2004). Its strength is that it helps to distinguish between the myriad influences on violence while at the same time providing a framework for understanding how they interact. The model assists in examining factors that influence behaviour – or that increase the risk of committing (or being a victim of) violence – by dividing them into four levels:

1. biological and personal history

2. close relationships

3. community contexts

4. broad societal factors.

The first level identifies *biological and personal history* factors that influence how individuals behave and increase their likelihood of becoming a victim or perpetrator of violence. Examples of factors that can be measured or traced include demographic characteristics (age, education, income), psychological or personality disorders, substance abuse, and a history of behaving aggressively or experiencing abuse. For example, involvement in violent or delinquent behaviour before the age of 13 years is a significant individual factor, and such children are more likely to become more seriously aggressive teenagers (Stattin and Magnusson 1989). Impulsivity, aggressive attitudes or beliefs, and low educational achievement have also been associated with later violence (Henry *et al.* 1996).

The second level looks at *close relationships*, such as those with family, friends, intimate partners and peers, and explores how these relationships increase the risk of being a victim or perpetrator of violence. In youth violence, for example, experiencing harsh physical punishment or witnessing violence in the home, lack of supervision and monitoring by parents, and associating with delinquent peers are important relationship factors (Farrington 1998). Violence usually occurs within the context of social interactions as part of a youth culture or lifestyle, and acts as a means of proving one's loyalty to the peer group and being accepted by it. Most young people are not specialists in violent offending; rather, their lifestyle provides a variety of opportunities for getting involved in different types of offending (McVie 2001).

The third level explores the *community contexts* in which social relationships occur, such as schools, workplaces and neighbourhoods, and seeks to identify the characteristics of these settings that increase the risk for violence. Risk at this level may be influenced by factors such as residential mobility (e.g. whether people in a neighbourhood tend to stay for a long time or move frequently), population density, high levels of unemployment, or the existence of a local drug trade or gangs. Research on other community and societal factors shows that young people living in neighbourhoods and communities with high levels of crime and poverty are at greater risk of violence (Farrington 1998). For some young people, adopting a tough, aggressive approach is regarded as an unavoidable aspect of life growing up in a deprived area and is something they are explicitly taught from a young age.

The fourth level looks at the *broad societal factors* that help create a climate in which violence is encouraged or inhibited. These include the availability of weapons and social and cultural norms. Such norms include those that give priority to parental rights over child welfare, those that regard suicide as a matter of individual choice instead of a preventable act of violence, those that entrench male dominance over women and children, those that support the use of excessive force by police against citizens, and those that support political conflict. Larger societal factors also include the health, economic, educational and social policies that help to maintain economic or social inequality between groups in society. Moreover, rates of youth violence rise in times of armed conflict and repression, and when the whole of society is caught up in social and political change.

The ecological perspective also highlights how factors at each level are strengthened or modified by factors at another. Thus, for example, a young person with an aggressive personality is more likely to act violently in a family or community that habitually resolves conflict through violence than if he or she were in a more peaceful environment. Besides helping to clarify the causes of violence and their complex interactions, the ecological model also suggests that in order to prevent violence it is necessary to act across several different levels at the same time. This includes, for example:

- addressing individual risk factors and taking steps to modify individual risk behaviours

- influencing close personal relationships and working to create healthy family environments, as well as providing professional help and support for dysfunctional families

- monitoring public places such as schools, workplaces and neighbourhoods and taking steps to address problems that might lead to violence

- addressing gender inequality and adverse cultural attitudes and practices

- addressing the larger cultural, social and economic factors that contribute to violence and taking steps to change them, including measures to close the gap between the rich and poor and to ensure equitable access to goods, services and opportunities.

The ecological perspective also explains why, in terms of the research on effective responses to young people and violence, that multi-dimensional interventions show most promise.

One example of this approach with an ongoing research base is multisystemic therapy (MST). This is a family- and community-based treatment for young people with complex clinical, social and educational problems, such as violent behaviour. Multisystemic therapists work in close partnership with the young person's family and community, in order to strengthen protective factors known to reduce the risk of future offending and anti-social behaviour, including aggression and acts of violence. Multisystemic therapy is currently the approach with the strongest evidence base in terms of effectiveness (Carr

2005). Similarly, evaluation studies carried out by the US Department of Justice Office of Juvenile Justice and Delinquency Prevention (OJJDP) into the prevention of gang violence identify the need for five key strategies around community mobilization, social intervention (including programmes), provision of social opportunities, enforcement and coordinated working between involved agencies (Pitts 2008).

The relevance of an individualized, specialized programme such as Choosing Non-Violence aimed specifically at the individual perpetrator of violence needs not to lose sight of the bigger picture that sees violence as a public health issue needing to be continually addressed across different levels. Decisions to offer a young person involvement within the Choosing Non-Violence programme need to be made within the wider ecological framework and hopefully as part of a package of interventions relevant to the young person's wider circumstances, needs and difficulties.

Programme theory base

Whilst recognizing the ecologically informed context of violence, the Choosing Non-Violence programme explicitly incorporates a range of theoretical perspectives in seeking to influence each young person towards pro-social, non-violent future behaviour.

Primarily, it encompasses the *restorative ethos*. To this end, it will work with the young person in a way that encourages him or her to consistently consider the impact of their violence on others, the harm it has caused and how they can demonstrate their commitment to trying to repair this harm. The process cannot be too tightly scripted. Although the theoretical perspectives outlined below will influence the content and structure of the programme in significant ways, ultimately it is about trying to encourage a more creative, improvised and individualized approach in helping each young person come up with something that works to restore the harm caused by their violence.

Another theoretical layer is around *change and motivation* theory. Andrews and Bonta (2003) state that in the field of criminal justice, evidence-based practice as outlined by criminologists has recommended that justice staff be responsive to motivational issues with offenders (quoted in Clark 2005). This reinforces the need to have a collaborative, empathic relationship with each young person, trying to give him or her as much ownership as possible in terms of finding ways of sorting out difficulties (Miller and Rollnick 2002).

Motivational interviewing theory informs this process in terms of recognizing the normalcy of ambivalence, resistance and blockages in how young people may view their violence. The approach will guide facilitators to find strategies that avoid argumentation, roll with resistance, build self-efficacy and develop the necessary edge to encourage the young person into meaningful reflection and dialogue. In other words, this approach encourages facilitators to develop styles that are 'respectful, acknowledge choices and ambivalence, and do not increase resistance' (Baer and Peterson 2002, p.322). Fundamental to this will be the need to focus on the young person's own life goals as motivating factors for the intervention; it is essential therefore to assess his or her own goals, life priorities and aims for the intervention (Ward and Maruna 2007). It is important to focus on these and, through the narrative approaches referred to below, help the young person recognize that there may be other ways to work towards these goals other than through violence.

Solution-focused and *strength-based approaches* can further assist in building the young person's confidence and self-esteem around situations that they have handled positively. These approaches caution against explaining and categorizing violent behaviour, on the grounds that it is not necessary to understand a problem to arrive at a solution. 'It is more profitable to concentrate on competencies rather than deficiencies, strengths rather than deficits, and safety rather than risk' (Milner and Myers 2007, p.130).

The Choosing Non-Violence programme content seeks to identify, emphasize, highlight and reinforce the young person's own abilities and strengths. At its simplest, it holds on to a belief in the capacity of young people to discover their own workable solutions to their problems. The aim is to try to find the seeds of solutions in the young person's current repertoire, seeking those occasions or exceptions, however small or rare, when the problem is less acute in order to identify something that the young person is thinking or doing that is helping deal with the problem in less violent ways. It is hoped that this will enhance the young person's sense of purpose and self-efficacy in relation to moving away from violence (Rutter, Giller and Hagell 1998).

The *narrative therapy model* assists in providing a way to explore the young person's violent episode that does not shame, blame or seek justification. This approach stresses the importance of the young person as a unique individual and provides a method in trying to separate him or her from their 'problem' behaviour. It offers a way to allow the young person to externalize his or her violence, to step back from it, to create some space between themselves and the problem, and look at it in a range of different ways to help them to see the role it has played in their lives. Ultimately, it is saying that the problem is the problem, the person is not the problem, and in the programme the aim will be to create a 'space between person and problem, [where] responsibility, choice and personal agency tend to expand' (Freeman, Epston and Lobovits 1997, p.8).

Finally, the *cognitive-behavioural* perspective encourages the young person to focus on the here and now of his or her behaviour, how they are deciding it, how they manage their thinking and feelings and how each of these relates to the other and to their actions.

In this sense, the programme will focus as much as possible on the violent act itself and the immediate situation giving rise to it. This approach tends to yield more practical suggestions for preventive action than focusing on more remote risk factors (Ward and Maruna).

Cognitive-behavioural programmes have been implemented globally, mainly with adults, and have been demonstrated to be effective in altering thinking processes associated with aggression (Goldstein *et al.* 2004). The Youth Justice Agency in England and Wales has identified research-based literature that highlights the usefulness of cognitive-behavioural approaches and the importance of challenging the young person's reasoning as much as his or her behaviour (Youth Justice Board 2005).

It is not possible to provide detailed outlines of the various theoretical elements referred to above that inform the programme. Indeed there may be a sense, and a danger, of the kitchen sink being thrown at the young person in terms of the underlying eclecticism of the programme. Facilitators will need to get to grips with these various approaches and see where each fits within the various sessions. Each will have its part to play. For example, the restorative ethos is foundational and will give a focus to many of the sessions. However, the claim that by just facing up to harm caused and taking responsibility will, on its own, produce positive behaviour change is not plausible. Each young person will need to be helped and coached in how to deal with the conflict situations that arise in his or her life. Analysis of situations, rehearsals of how to deal with issues and identification of necessary skills in avoiding violence will all need to be covered, reflecting the other theoretical approaches referred to above.

It is important that programme facilitators have some understanding of the inter-relationships of the different theoretical perspectives used and follow the guidance given in each of the sessions. However, the essence of the programme will be the ability of the facilitator to work positively with the young person, to have a real understanding of and empathy for the young person's situation and circumstances and to work with him or her in a purposeful, planned way as outlined within the session guidance. Without this therapeutic relationship, there is a danger of a 'dry, overly didactic approach that alienates most clients and ultimately has the opposite effect to what is intended' (Ward and Maruna 2007, p.130).

It has been shown time and time again that it is not just what is done, not the therapies, but the interaction between the two human beings that is critical (Hamer 2006). Successful outcomes are strongly influenced by effective facilitators who are warm, optimistic, enthusiastic, creative and imaginative, and who use their personal influence through the quality of interaction directly with young people (Trotter 1999). Putting it another way, an approach that is engaged, relational and therapeutic will be maintained as this tends to have more successful outcomes). It is a person-centred, empowering and holistic approach embodying choice and flexibility; it is non-labelling and non-judgemental and recognizes young people's strengths.

Nevertheless, the facilitator should have a clear sense of purpose and direction in each session. Ultimately, the facilitation is aimed at helping the young person come to his or her view of what caused their behaviour and what is needed to change it. It is being clear that the role is not to counsel the young person or provide deep insights to try and explain the violence. Rather it is about focusing on his or her thinking and behaviour, offering purposeful participatory activities that take account of learning style, such as art, music, games and activities.

These are the types of approaches that will increase the chances of the young person moving towards more positive attitudes and behaviours (Bonta 2004). From this, and to meet the restorative requirement of the programme, the young person will work towards presenting the outcome of the work and their plan of action, including a letter of apology (if relevant) to show how they intend to choose a more non-violent lifestyle. Ultimately, the vision is one of the young person taking some steps away from a life of fear and violence to one marked with greater understanding, compassion and pro-social behaviour (Chapman 2000).

Specific issues for programme design and delivery

Gender issues

Seymour (2009) argues that all violence is ultimately gendered violence. There certainly is enough evidence to demand that careful consideration is given to gender issues in relation to the delivery of the programme.

The evidence continues to suggest strongly that violence (particularly serious violence) is still an overwhelmingly male activity, and that whilst there may be an increase in young women's involvement in violence, the vast majority of female offending is non-violent (Stanko 2002). There are some similarities between males and females and their respective relationship with violence. Among both genders the strongest predictors of violence are having violent friends, involvement in non-violent offending and having a girlfriend/ boyfriend. Weaker predictors are 'hanging around' frequently, adversarial contact with the police and experience of violent victimization (WHO 2004).

Violent boys are *very similar* to non-violent boys, which, coupled with their high prevalence of violence, suggests that it is a normal expression of masculine identity at this age, which indeed is part of the problem. More and more the inter-relationships between shame and masculinity, and in particular the limited capacity of some men to process complex emotions such as shame, have emerged as significant factors in understanding violence (Jones 2008).

A greater understanding of how females involved in violence differ from males and how risk and protective factors may affect females differently is crucial for implementing intervention and prevention programmes that target girls and women (Hart *et al.* 2007, p.368). Violent girls are *very different* from both non-violent girls and violent boys (McVie 2001). The prevalence of experiences of sexual, physical and emotional abuse in the histories of women who have committed violent offences is demonstrated in the literature (Batchelor 2005). In addition, the evidence also suggests that 'most of the violence that girls and young women experience, as both perpetrators and victims, takes place within either the family or friendship group' (Batchelor 2010, p.409).

This issue, helping women to begin to see connections between their past experiences of victimization and their current behaviours, needs to be taken account of in the programme design. Some research has supported the use of separate programmes for males and females that would be tailored to fit their individual needs (Hart *et al.* 2007). As another commentator has put it, 'any work targeting young women who have committed violent offences needs to take account of their gendered experiences of substance misuse, abuse, suicide, self-harm, family relationships and responsibilities...the worker must assist young women to develop an understanding of their victimisation and should encourage them to address the strong feelings of anger and frustration that contribute to offending behaviour' (Batchelor 2005, p.371).

Those delivering the programme need to bring flexibility and discretion in giving space to young women to explore these issues in helping them begin to see their connections to current violence. Programmes for young women are successful where they 'focus on relationships with other people and offer ways to master their lives whilst keeping their relationships intact' (Belknap, Dunn and Holsinger 1997, p.23).

The programme design seeks to offer space and discretion for the facilitator in working with young women as required. It also allows for a more structured approach, which, if helpful, may be followed more closely in working with young males.

Learning difficulties

The issue of learning difficulties also needs to be addressed in programme design. Studies conducted on learning difficulties and violent behaviours have found that violence increased as learning difficulties increased (Blum, Svetaz and Ireland 2000). Juveniles with learning difficulties may not have the social or cognitive skills needed to resist involvement in delinquent behaviour, and they may be treated differently because of their difficulties (Morrison and Cosden 1997). Again, facilitator discretion, skill and flexibility in finding ways to engage with young people with a range of learning difficulties will be required. The material needs to be meaningful and to connect with the particular young person.

Alcohol and drugs

Alcohol and drug misuse are significant risk factors for involvement in youth violence and also need to be considered in the delivery of the programme. Many studies (mostly in developed countries) have specifically examined alcohol-related violence and its associated risk factors (Blum *et al.* 2000).

Males are more likely than females to be both perpetrators and victims of alcohol-related youth violence. However, in some countries harmful alcohol consumption has been associated with disproportionate increases in levels of violent behaviour among girls despite their overall levels of alcohol and violence being generally lower than male counterparts.

Those who start drinking at an earlier age, drink frequently and drink large quantities have been shown to be at increased risk of being both perpetrators and victims of violence. Research among schoolchildren in Switzerland found that having been drunk more than once was positively associated with perpetration of bullying and violence, yet reduced the risks of being a victim of bullying, particularly amongst socially integrated individuals.

The research indicates that much alcohol-related violence is reactive, triggered by events such as an argument or an advance by one person towards another's sexual partner. Young men explain their aggressive responses to these events as necessary for defending their honour and retaining the respect of their peers; however, fighting for fun is also a common reason given for initiating violence.

Among young males, drinking may be part of the preparation for participating in such violence. Alcohol can also facilitate aggression by increasing confidence and willingness to take risks, making people more aroused and emotional, and reducing their ability to consider the consequences of their behaviour.

Managing the risk of violence

Risk assessment and management run through modern life like blood through veins. Our world is now dominated by risk-related issues and fears. We have seen that even with the most sophisticated security and monitoring systems available, disasters can sometimes occur without warning. In working with violence, risk issues will always be there and will present challenges in terms of how best to assess levels of danger and harm.

The profile of the violence used by each young person will vary. It will go across a continuum of aggressive acts from bullying and physical fighting, to more serious forms of assault and worse. It may be the young person who is willingly involved in gang fights and related conflict. It may be the young person who attacks someone because of their race, religion or sexuality. It may be a young person in care who has experienced significant past traumas and who within a complex web of relationships carries out violence towards a member of staff that is extreme and worrying (Child Care NI 2000). It may be the young person being threatening and violent to a parent or carer. It may be a young person whose violence and aggression appears to be of a reactive nature in terms of responding to something done to them and motivated by fear and frustration and where the young person may be out of control. On the other hand, it may be a more proactive type of aggression, which may be motivated more by manipulation and intimidation and where the young person may appear to be very much in control (Bath 1999).

Each young person's violence profile needs to be considered carefully in terms of its level of risk. The majority will be those who engage in violent behaviour over limited periods of time, during adolescence, having shown little or no evidence of problem behaviour as children. Such 'adolescence-limited offenders' are often looking for excitement (LeBlanc and Frechette 1989). Their violent acts are often committed in the company of a group of friends, although the presence of alcohol, drugs or weapons enhances the likelihood that injuries or deaths will be associated with violence. Nevertheless, in all probability, most of these young people are likely to move away from such behaviour, and this process can be stimulated and encouraged through their positive engagement with a restorative process and programme of personal work.

However, some children exhibit problem behaviour in early childhood that gradually escalates to more severe forms of aggression as they enter adolescence, and typically continues into adulthood (Stattin and Magnusson 1996). These young people may well have come from problem families, have had disrupted school careers and as adults will have troubled relationships with others and become 'life course persistent offenders' (Jones 2008). They will present greater issues of risk, and from some of these will emerge those young people, mostly males, who may become both the principal perpetrators and victims of homicide.

To a certain degree, it may then be possible to compartmentalize young people into particular risk categories, but this needs to be carried out with great care. Assessing and managing risk is an inexact science, an 'indeterminate (uncertain) process' (Ward and Maruna 2007). It remains the case that accurate prediction of violent behaviour by a particular person is still out of reach. Whilst it is possible to identify various factors that correlate with the potential for violence, it also needs to be recognized that 'any assumption that people who are violent are similar to each other and different from non-violent people is…fatally flawed' (Milner and Myers 2007, p.135).

Recognizing the complexity and limitations with risk assessment, the programme nevertheless may need to align itself with the host agency's risk assessment procedures and protocols. The fact that the programme comprises approximately 12–18 hours of intervention means that it would not be sufficient for those young people considered to be at high risk of causing serious harm to others. There will also be the need for the programme to be located within a broader package of interventions to help tackle other risk-related areas. In addition, serious domestic violence, community violence or violence motivated by hatred towards particular people because of their ethnicity, religion, disability, sexuality, etc. will also require accountability and sanction from society – education can only go so far!

Finally, in relation to risk, there may also be the issue that some of the young people may present with anger outbursts and overt aggressive behaviour. Host agency health and safety procedures need to be in place to take account of this possibility in terms of location, back up staff available, etc. At the same time, it is important that the facilitator is not unduly alarmed by an exposure to anger. Remaining calm provides counterbalancing reassurance, and it also prevents giving off cues that may be misread as threat signals by an angry person (Novaco and Chemtob 1998). It is important not to take it personally. An outburst may even provide an unexpected opportunity to teach anger-coping skills.

For the young person it may be that anger may have got them what they wanted in certain situations, and it may be difficult to relinquish this sense of control and effectiveness. Of course, if the young person's anger or aggression is not possible to manage and it is causing distress or being disruptive to the work, then a supported withdrawal from the programme will be required. A general protective factor is the ethos of respect and acceptance built into the programme and the approach which strives to ensure that no young person is placed in a position where they are embarrassed, humiliated or degraded.

Working with different types of violence

Dag Hammarskjöld, a former Secretary General of the United Nations, when talking about violence within another context, used the analogy of the gardener who would not plant weeds in one part of the garden if trying to avoid them in other parts! The point is well made. It would be unlikely for someone to be violent within one area of their life and it not to be an issue in other areas. The individual young person engaging with the Choosing Non-Violence programme may bring various examples of the use of violence in his or her life. The programme aims to assist in the prevention of all types of interpersonal violence by young people, rather than focusing on individual sub-types of interpersonal violence, such as family violence, gang violence, cybernet bullying, ethnically motivated violence, sectarian violence, sexual violence, elder abuse, etc.

Specialized prevention efforts that focus on a single sub-type of interpersonal violence are becoming more common; yet evidence is increasing that underlying the different sub-types is a set of common causes and cross-cutting risk factors. The need for more specialized interventions may well become clear through the engagement with some young people. However, the programme will seek to help each young person address common themes and factors in his or her interpersonal violence and will strive to contribute to a reduction in all forms of interpersonal violence, particularly if the programme can be delivered within the multi-systemic framework referred to earlier (WHO 2004).

Delivering the programme

The Choosing Non-Violence programme reflects the reality that there is no universal agreement as to why some people are violent. In one sense, it sets that question aside. It asks each young person to look at where he or she is, at this particular point in their lives, and where they want to get to in terms of their use of violence. Can the young person take some responsibility for dealing with it and moving towards a less violent future? It is educational and will seek to encourage each individual to fully explore their behaviours, the consequences for their victims, themselves, their families and communities and to seek if possible to restore the harm done. It will explore with the young person the controlled and sometimes uncontrolled use of violence. It will seek to help the young person to change negative and destructive mindsets and motivation around violence; as well as affecting him or her on a level of emotion and empathy. It will also strive to promote the development of positive behaviours resting on respect, acceptance and tolerance and the acquisition of new skills to reduce the likelihood of violent behaviour.

The challenge for those delivering the Choosing Non-Violence programme is to acquire a sense of the perspectives presented and use these to connect with the young person in a committed, skilful and insightful way. 'Effective practice needs to fit the individual person, rather than the person fit the practice' (Milner and Myers 2007, p.178). This will be within the capability of qualified social, youth, community, educational and mental health workers provided with ongoing training and support. To this end, a significant amount of material has been outlined in this section and additional guidance and ideas are provided within each of the sessions. In addition, potential facilitators of the programme who wish to deepen their understanding of its foundational knowledge and theoretical base can access this in the publications listed below.

Further reading

Chapman, T. (2000) *Time to Grow*. Lyme Regis: Russell House Publishing.

Gilligan, J. (2000) *Violence: Reflections on Our Deadliest Epidemic*. London: Jessica Kingsley Publishers.

Jones, D.W. (2008) *Understanding Criminal Behaviour: Psychosocial Approaches to Criminality*. Cullompton: Willan.

Miller, W.R. and Rollnick, S. (2002) *Motivational Interviewing: Preparing People for Change*. New York, NY: Guilford Press.

Milner, J. and Myers, S. (2007) *Working with Violence*. Basingstoke: Palgrave Macmillan.

Ward, T. and Maruna, S. (2007) *Rehabilitation Beyond the Risk Paradigm*. London: Routledge.

World Health Organization (2004) *Preventing Violence: A Guide to Implementing the Recommendations of the World Report on Violence and Health*. Geneva: WHO.

Youth Justice Board (2005) *Risk and Protective Factors*. London: Youth Justice Board.

Supporting the programme

The author is committed to supporting those wishing to use the Choosing Non-Violence programme. To this end a range of services are available:

- training programmes to agencies on delivery and facilitation of the programme

- consultancy services to those delivering the programme.

Contact through email to gheery@ntlworld.com or +44 (0)7806 789438. Feedback on use of the programme would be greatly appreciated.

Chapter 2
Facilitating the Choosing Non-Violence Programme

'Work done without creativity is simply brutality.'

Mark Hamer (2006, p.11)

The Choosing Non-Violence programme comprises 12 sessions, each lasting approximately 1–1½ hours. As indicated in the figure below, each session has a similar structure with four distinct elements. In terms of learning theory, the sessions are designed to maximize the young person's engagement with, and concentration on, the task. They will work in bursts of 15 minutes or so with a short break between segments. This will also allow the facilitators some discretion in the time allocated to each element and to build some flexibility into the programme.

Element 1 Welcome and check-in	Element 2	B R E A K	Element 3	Element 4 Taking care of yourself, and closure

Elements 1 and 4, and the closure, will be identical for all of the sessions.

Element 1: Welcome and check-in

Beginnings are vital and the 'Welcome and check-in' is intended to be warm, positive and affirming – to welcome those who have attended.

As well as serving as a way of welcoming the young person each week, it is used to communicate the content and objectives of each session: agreeing how the work will go forward and also giving the young person a chance to think about his or her motivation for doing this work and what may help or hinder them in doing so. The objectives for each session are outcome-based and each element within the session will relate to one or more of these.

Outline briefly the purpose and objectives of the session you are running (the objectives for each session are given in bullet form at the start of each session described in Part 2). This is first of all about making the young person feel comfortable and giving him or her a clear idea of what he or she is getting into as a result of the decision taken to try to do something about their use of violence and to attend the session.

The aim is to break down the overall challenge of helping the young person move away from using violence into smaller, more achievable tasks; in other words, to facilitate participants to work on focused, goal-limited objectives, rather than on a global violence problem that can otherwise seem impenetrable and insolvable (Novaco and Chemtob 1998).

At the beginning of the very first session (i.e. Session 1, Element 1), there will be several additional things to do. You will need to introduce yourself and share a little about your background and experiences. It is important to stress your interest and commitment to working alongside young people in helping them to undertake the work. It can also be helpful to point out that nearly everyone has to look at issues around violence and aggression at some point in their lives.

At the start of Session 1, participants should also be asked to sign an agreement or 'contract' that outlines how the work should be done. A template copy is provided in the handout on p.53. This agreement addresses the points below:

- *mutual respect* between young person and facilitator

- *acceptance* of young person's views

- *good participation and involvement* by the young person and the facilitator in all parts of the programme (which should also cover requirements to turn up in an alcohol/drug free state, switch off mobiles, etc.)

- *confidentiality* as much as possible – the facilitator needs to make clear again the limits to this through a clear statement along the lines of 'I don't want to know anything you don't want to tell me. What you tell me is significant. I will take what you say very seriously. If you tell me about any abuse or serious crime that you have suffered or have committed or that would give me concerns about your safety, I will have to tell the appropriate authorities.'

For subsequent sessions, Element 1: Welcome and check-in presents an opportunity for the participant to 'check in'.

The 'check-in' involves the participant taking a few moments to reflect on how violence is playing out in their lives. Without necessarily getting into too much detail, can they communicate how big a problem their use of violent or aggressive behaviour has been since the last session? They should be encouraged to spend just a minute at the end of every day (not just the days they are attending the programme) to consider how aggressive they have been, and to keep a record of their aggression (see handout 'Checking in,' p.58).

At the start of each new session they will have the chance to make a brief statement and give their own personal score in relation to their level of violence and aggression. More importantly, each young person will also be asked to select a situation in which they could have been violent but chose not to be. This could be an occasion when they were embarrassed, shamed, angry or annoyed and would normally have been violent. It may be hard for them to come up with examples of this, but it is trying to help them see any little glimpse of something that may take them away from the dominant violence story.

Any action, feeling, statement, quality, desire, thought, belief, ability, commitment that contradicts their habitual problematic move towards a violent aggressive response should be reinforced. Can the facilitator help the young person to see that sometimes they do have some control over their behaviour and are not always overwhelmed by feelings that just explode, or that there may be gateways to other stories that are not just about violence? The key thing is that the events need to be something that the young person gives significance to. The facilitator should never fall into the trap of persuading or trying to convince the young person that something is positive. This may build resistance and strengthen the problematic behaviour. Only the individual can evaluate his or her own life.

Other questions that may be helpful to discuss at the check-in include:

- Have there been times since we last met that the aggression is not as bad as usual, when it is less dominating or bossy?

- How have you managed to stop the behaviour from getting worse?

- Is there a story you could tell me about a time when you resisted the behaviour and did what you wanted instead?

- What has changed since the last session and how did you do that?

Where the young person is identifying exceptions to the presence of violence these should be recognized and affirmed. Exceptions are the first sign of safety. Even if they are being discounted as chance events (e.g. 'I don't know – it just happened') or the results of someone else's behaviour (e.g. 'He didn't wind me up as much'), the young person's avoidance of violence should be affirmed.

As the sessions progress and positive examples are presented, the young person can be helped to analyse this control in more detail to try to pick out what he or she is doing so they can do it again and build upon progress. It is also important to try to make a connection between the young person's efforts in choosing not to be violent and their goals in life, and to show how this may be helping them move towards a better future for themselves and those they are in relationships with.

So, the check-in is vital as a way of reinforcing the continuity of the learning process. It encourages the young person to monitor he or she is doing.

Elements 2 and 3: The Choosing Non-Violence curriculum

These differ for each session and are constructed using a variety of approaches as indicated below.

The aim is to relate to the young person's particular learning style and preference, whether this be visual, aural, through reading and writing or of a more participatory active mode. It is important to clarify the needs of the participant in relation to literacy before commencing, and then to deliver the material in the way that best suits his or her learning needs.

The participant should be advised that written work will not be a demand of the programme but it is a helpful aid for those who prefer to do so. He or she can use a notebook for this purpose. Session handouts can also be provided for participants as a resource. These are provided in most of the sessions as a tool for the facilitator to help with the work and can be used, or not, in whatever way best connects with the young person's learning style.

As indicated in the previous section, the overall approach is designed to provide opportunities for the young person to address his or her behaviour in a safe way. To this end, various approaches will be used in each of the sessions:

- *Information giving*: The facilitator will present information to the young person, which can be done verbally, in writing or using audio visual approaches. The onus is on the facilitator to get the key messages across in as clear a way as possible for the young person.

- *Two-way discussions*: These will usually follow on from the above, and will involve the young person in discussing issues raised by the input with the facilitator.

- *Exercises*: More experiential activities including sculpts, games, role play, drawing, visits, collage work, and so on, again depending on the particular young person.

- *Individual work*: This will comprise time for the young person to relate material to his or her own situation, to complete drawings, self-assessments, handouts, plans, and so on, which they may wish to keep or use to reflect on some of the implications and learning for themselves.

Element 4: Taking care of yourself

This element is identical in all sessions and acts both as a relaxing way to finish off the session but also as a way of introducing a wider focus on helping the young person begin to think about wider lifestyle issues: it is designed to help empower the young person with some coping skills for self-care.

This short element centres on a relaxing or enjoyable activity to bring the young person out of what may have been more intense personal material earlier in the session. The element also seeks in a low-key way to flag up the importance of looking after ourselves. It aims to encourage the young person to take seriously the need to look after themselves, physically, mentally, emotionally and spiritually in their wider lives. Opportunities to expose the young person to positive community experiences and resources should be seized upon.

In practical terms, it can consist of a range of positive experiential and/or creative exercises around relaxation (breathing, muscular and visualizations), drawing and art work, or music. For some it may simply be a cup of tea or listening to a favourite piece of music. You can compile additional resources and exercises as you continue to run the programme, and receive input from the young people to supplement the ideas in this resource.

The specific nature of the activities can be selected by the facilitator based on what they think is best suited to the young person – the exercises listed in Appendix 1 are simply suggestions (adapted and included with permission from Heery 2006).

Following the activity, Element 4 should end with a short closure aimed at encouraging the young person briefly to identify one piece of learning and to come up with a way to 'practise' what has been learned before the next session.

Element 4: Taking care of yourself seeks to provide experiences to the young person that recognize and affirm him or her as a unique special individual whose needs for physical, psychological, emotional and spiritual self-care are important. It is about recognizing the holistic needs of the young person, and also emphasizing the importance of self-care and stress management in providing a more stable foundation from which the young person's efforts to choose non-violence and to manage anger and aggression can be built up and sustained.

Summary

Ultimately, the intention is to provide a positive learning experience for the young person. This is more likely to happen when 'what' they are learning includes all of who they are. Learning is successful and change is more certain when their head (knowing), their heart (valuing) and their hands and feet (doing) are all engaged in a healthy purpose (www.chebucto.ns.ca/CommunitySupport/Men4Change).

Recognizing Hamer's stark challenge at the start of the chapter, the critical task is for the facilitator to be creative and flexible in working through each of the elements of the programme in ways that are responsive to the individual young person's learning style. For example, with some young people with a learning difficulty there may be a need to spread the elements of a particular session over more than one meeting. The principle of responsivity needs to be at the heart of the programme, in that the facilitator should use a style and mode of intervention that engages the interest of the young person and takes into account his or her relevant characteristics, such as cognitive ability, learning style and values (Andrews and Bonta 2003).

What follows is a chapter dedicated to explaining the broader context of implementing the programme and its evaluation. If you prefer, you can skip this section to the programme itself, but I recommend revisiting it once you find yourself in a position to reflect on how you will be implementing the programme.

Chapter 3
Delivering an Ethical and Effective Programme

'Violence is the voice of the unheard.'

Martin Luther King

Martin Luther King recognized in his speeches and writings that violence often came from those with little power and influence within society. Of course the question could be asked as to whether or not violence is an expression of powerlessness or power, or both. It is certainly a complex phenomenon. '[There is] very rarely a single explanation, or a single solution for the problems that confront the mish mash of genes, experience, and environment from which all human beings are forged' (Newman *et al.* 2005, p.10). Consequently, the degree to which a narrowly focused, short-term intervention designed to counteract proscribed beliefs, attitudes and behaviours among at-risk young people impacts on their relationship with violence needs to be considered carefully (Pitts 2008).

In this section, Choosing Non-Violence's appropriateness, effectiveness and future contribution to violence reduction work will be considered, and three main issues addressed.

First, there is the bigger picture of the social and economic situations experienced by many potential participants. This raises questions as to the appropriateness of putting so much energy, enthusiasm and expertise into such an individualized approach.

Second, given that a reasonable case can be made for the programme as a useful intervention, then there are responsibilities on agencies and individuals to ensure it is delivered in an ethical and effective manner.

Finally, if the programme appears to be helpful to some young people then what is the best way to demonstrate this, gather an evidence base and sustain its future growth?

The bigger picture

Various commentators in differing contexts have pointed out the dangers of some 'helping' interventions regressing to the individualization of wider social problems. Structural issues of inequality, discrimination and their like are ignored and the onus is put on people to sort out their own problems whatever the circumstances they are experiencing. There are strong arguments for asserting that violence within society relates mostly to social and structural factors and needs to be addressed at that level.

Some would go further and challenge the integrity of such approaches, with one referring to a 'small army of shameless, entrepreneurial, academic and private sector claim makers who stalk the youth justice system…with the inexorable logic of the individualizing imperative to abstract the cheapest, most readily do-able elements…to endeavour to market something that works' (Pitts 2008, p.162).

Can these types of criticism be fairly put against this programme? The point has already been made in Chapter 1 that young people in trouble with violence need a multi-disciplinary and multi-dimensional approach. The bottom line is that intervention strategies need to be based on a 'comprehensive holistic assessment, addressing the needs of children and young people as well as parents and the communities they live in; choosing methods, approaches, and services that will help with many difficulties, such as poverty, social isolation, mental-health problems, dysfunctional marital relationships, family violence, substance misuse and so on' (Iwaniec 2003, p.55).

However, within such a context, the crucial need remains to provide the opportunity and space for each young person to be encouraged to take a long hard look at their own behaviour, their decisions and emotional reactions, to help them begin to think about their own goals and hopes and whether they can see these beyond violence. The approach must rest on a value base that recognizes the uniqueness and importance of each individual in his or her own right, and not just as a social category.

Ultimately, it is about making a commitment to, and seeking to empower the young person to be helped in looking at their own situation and circumstances. The goal is to help them make their own choices in regard to their future relationship with violence. It will also seek to enable them to see the consequences of violent actions on others and encourage them to reflect on the need to make good the harm that may have been caused. Programmes such as Choosing Non-Violence have their place in empowering young people to achieve some sense of meaning, responsibility and ownership of how they deal with the difficult circumstances they encounter.

Programme effectiveness and integrity

The points made above do not, on their own, provide a justification for using scarce resources to provide this programme. There is also a responsibility on those delivering it to ensure that it is done so as intended; is managed efficiently; and that facilitators receive sufficient support.

Tight design

This manual seeks to contribute to and enhance the design of the programme. It sets out clearly its underpinning value base as well as its knowledge and skill requirements. Each session is clearly structured to move the young person through a process of learning and change. Clear tasks within each session are aligned to meet defined objectives that come together to meet the overall aims of the programme. It is important to have the material in a manual so that the integrity of the intervention can be evaluated and replicated, as discussed below.

However, there will always be some tension in using a manual-based programme. There is a danger of being dogmatic about the programme and insisting that it is delivered in precisely the same way to allow for programme integrity, consistency and research. The challenge is to create enough space to allow for creativity and flexibility in how it is delivered to different individuals and groups so that it is grounded in their own realities, communities and cultures, without losing its essential elements. 'We need a balance of clear manual guidelines, possibilities for improvisation and space for individual therapist differences – a difficult task' (Herbert 2000, p.87).

This is all the more critical given the theoretical mix of the programme, the complexities in terms of how gender appears to relate to violence, as well as the wide range of personalities, learning styles and cultural backgrounds of participating young people.

Sound management

The second important element in programme integrity centres on the responsibility of any agency that wishes to use Choosing Non-Violence to ensure that the organizational culture and structure is in tune with what is required. Agencies will need to recognize fully the commitment involved, and take the appropriate steps to ensure that they do the following:

- understand the Choosing Non-Violence programme and promote it properly

- procure appropriate funds, equipment and accommodation

- manage information about the programme

- support facilitators

- monitor its delivery

- evaluate and improve delivery if required

- build partnership and consultancy arrangements with other agencies.

Agencies may also be able to enhance the programme in various innovative and creative ways, particularly in developing a range of resources for the programme, such as examples of violence-related issues on DVD and resources for the 'Taking care of yourself' elements.

Skilled practitioners

Finally, there is an onus placed on the facilitators who wish to deliver Choosing Non-Violence to young people. Key issues for maintaining the integrity of the programme include the following:

- a commitment to the values of the programme

- an understanding of the knowledge base

- competence in 'supporting skills' (creating the right relationship to support change) and 'structuring skills' that keep the relationship focused on addressing the right issues in the right way.

This manual contains a sufficient basis of the above material to allow a committed facilitator to operate effectively in this area. However, given its broad theory base and the spectrum of violent behaviours that may be addressed, significant skill, discretion, patience and support will be required. Nevertheless, and as stated earlier, this type of intervention can be delivered by a wide range of people. It is significant, for example, that the Youth Justice Board in England and Wales has recommended that, in relation to who should facilitate managing offending behaviour programmes, staff members' personal skills and qualities should have a higher priority than their qualifications or professional background alone.

Research on the quality of staff involved in similar cognitive behavioural programmes concluded that such programmes should be facilitated by those interested in, and committed to, the work (Feilzer *et al.* 2004). Supportive supervision and/or coaching and mentoring from someone with more experience in this area may assist prospective facilitators increase their confidence and competence.

Evaluation and building the evidence base

Finally, there is the need to be clear about the outcomes of the intervention. Attempts to document the number, nature and scope of community-based violence-prevention programmes suggest that while many such programmes exist, there are very few that have used scientific data and evidence to inform their design.

With regard to this programme, the initial small-scale pilot provided anecdotal evidence of positive engagement with individual young people and this needs to be built on by gathering evidence of the longer-term outcomes related to a reduction in the use of violence. To this end, facilitators of this programme should consider evaluating the outcomes of the work. It is a valid and important task to commit themselves 'to undertake small-scale, agency-based evaluations of their own practice' (Thyer 1998, p.172). It is only through the gathering of detailed information and feedback from participants that a clearer picture may begin to emerge as to the degree to which the programme is associated with young people choosing less violence in their lives. For example, in relation to the issue of girls' involvement in violence 'much more evidence is needed to help us fully understand the extent, nature and gender specific dimensions of young women's involvement in violent offending' (Catch 22 2009, p.7).

Outcomes research carried out at agency or programme level does not usually require sophisticated experimental designs because the questions being asked are not sophisticated. Basically, they will centre on whether young people found the inputs helped them in moving towards less violence in their lives. This 'research' element needs to be built in from the start of the programme. 'Ethical research involves getting the informed consent of those you are going to interview, question, observe or take materials from. It involves reaching an agreement about the uses of the data, and how the analysis will be reported and disseminated' (Blaxter, Hughes and Tight 2001, p.158). An agreement could be made with the young person at the contracting stage for him or her to share their views on how helpful they found the work and perhaps to give some feedback on whether they have been able to keep any of their learning with them after the programme has been completed.

It is important to hear the voices of the young people at the receiving end of this intervention. Emphasis upon quantitative measurements, monopolized by researchers as experts, undermines the qualitative issues and excludes the voice of the service user (Jones, Cooper and Ferguson 2008). In evaluating other interventions, I have found that when young people are asked about the acceptability of using simple evaluation procedures to help assess the outcomes of practice, they mostly say they find such techniques acceptable. (A suggested evaluation form is provided in Appendix 2.)

Of course it is important to build in an independent element to the gathering of such information. This may involve using a colleague or a different agency. Purchasing independent research can be expensive, and whether or not it is possible to negotiate local arrangements with academic institutions or with community-development or social-care schemes needs to be explored. Finally, it is important that evaluative material is made as widely available as possible. This will provide a form of quality assurance in that it will lead to critical scrutiny and feedback from others interested in this area of work. It is also the case that locally conducted research is more likely to be perceived as relevant to practice (Newman *et al.* 2005).

Research also needs to reach the people on the ground, and then the policy-makers. This unfortunately does not happen enough with research in education, social care or criminal justice. Publicizing evaluations of practice may also assist others to benefit in terms of developing their own practice initiatives. Ultimately, a commitment to trying to measure and evaluate practice will assist in the ongoing process of theory building and the development of a body of empirical knowledge (Chapman and Hough 1998).

Conclusion

John Hume, a Nobel Peace Prize winner, struggled for many years in seeking to convince others to choose non-violent ways in dealing with political differences and conflict in Northern Ireland. He repeated over and over again the importance of finding peaceful ways to deal with differences and disagreements. A legacy of bitterness and hurt made it difficult for all to choose non-violent means to pursue their goals but, as the peace process has demonstrated, many have been able to do so. Similarly, in working with young people and violence, the reality of the situations in which they live can never be lost sight of. It will not be easy for some young people to choose non-violence. They have little choice with regard to many of the factors contributing to their use of violence; for example, traumatic experiences in their families of origin, poor and deprived neighbourhoods, limited educational or employment opportunities, and high levels of criminality within their communities.

Violence needs to be tackled continually at different levels within society, through coordinated social, educational, community and justice-based initiatives. However, part of this response also needs to involve purposeful and respectful engagement with the individual young person to encourage the choice of non-violence. In one sense this programme is about having a conversation with him or her about their use of violence. Through this they may be helped to become more aware of the harm it does to others and themselves, and encouraged and supported in finding ways and building the confidence and skills to choose non-violent pathways in their future lives. While this material originates from Northern Ireland, it is my belief that the approach is a universal one which would benefit any young person.

Much of this section has been aimed at those who wish to use the programme in its entirety, to ensure they have the necessary supports and framework to do so with integrity. For those working with young people from a position of respect and acceptance, but who choose to use this resource in a more limited way, it is offered very much in the spirit: take what helps and leave the rest.

Part 2
The Choosing Non-Violence Programme

Session 1
Choice!

The main objectives of the session are that the young person will:

- feel welcome, understand and agree to do the programme

- increase their understanding of what violence is

- consider their motivation to move away from using violence.

Content	Methods and process
Element 1. Welcome and check-in Welcome, introduction, objectives of the session and check-in.	Affirming and positive. Explain purpose, content and style of programme (p.36). Sign the contract (see p.53) (and, if required, clarify reason for doing the programme).
Element 2. What is violence? Working at reaching an agreed understanding of what violence is and also a sense of how widespread it is and how 'normal' it can appear.	Try to get a sense of what the young person's understanding of violence is – using the young person's own experiences and observations.

Break

Element 3. How big a deal is my violence? How 'ready, willing and able' is the young person to work at change and to choose not to be violent?	Explore with the young person his or her thinking and feelings about the violence they use in their lives, their ambivalence about it and whether or not they want to choose to move away from it. Relate this to the check-in (pp.37–38).

Element 4. Taking care of yourself	A short activity or exercise related to self-care, dealing with stress, relaxation, fun, etc. See Appendix 1 for selection, or can be decided with the young person.

Closure: Thank the young person for his or her participation; stress that the work is done, but as they get ready to leave just in a word or two let you know:

1. how they are feeling

2. one piece of learning that the young person will think about or 'practise' before the next session.

Handout: Agreement to do the Choosing Non-Violence programme

Purpose

The overall aim of the programme is to provide the opportunity for you to take responsibility for your violence and work towards developing a plan of action to make good the harm caused by the violence and reduce the likelihood of further violent behaviour.

Objectives

By the end of the programme you will:

- know more about violence and its effects

- learn and practise non-violent ways of dealing with difficult situations

- relate this to your future goals and what *you* want in your life

- try to make good any harm you have caused.

Contract

We will work together and treat each other with respect.

We will listen to each other's views and you will only have to talk about what you want to. What *you* say is significant and I will take it seriously.

If you say something about any abuse or serious crime that you have suffered or have committed or that would give concerns about your safety, I will have to tell the appropriate authorities.

You will come to the sessions on time, in an alcohol and drug free state and take part as well as you can.

Signed: . . . .

Session 1, Element 2: What is violence?

The World Health Organization has agreed that the definition of violence is the intentional use of physical force or power, threatened or actual, against oneself, another person, or against a group or community, that either results in or has a high likelihood of resulting in injury, death, psychological harm, mal-development or deprivation.

Rather than present the above definition, this element will involve the young person thinking through and coming to their own understanding of what violence is. The worksheet or something similar could be used as a prompt to help the young person identify the different forms of violence that they are aware of and also the fact that it is often a part of everyday life and so much so that much of it goes unnoticed and becomes normalized. Use the handout 'My experience of violence' to give the young person a sense of the amount of violence they have experienced in the past week.

Alternatively, the more experiential option of going out with the young person into his or her community to be shown where violence happens could be considered. Accompanying the young person around his or her area, listening to their stories of when and where violence occurs will not only bring to life the social-cultural context of their violence but will also give a strong message of trying to get a real understanding of the young person's situation and help build a positive working relationship.

From either of the above exercises agree with the young person his or her definition of violence bringing out its wide-ranging nature as indicated in WHO's definition above.

Handout: My experience of violence

	At school	At work	In the community	On TV/the internet	In magazines	At home	At the weekend
Disrespecting, putting down, slagging, dissing, etc.							
Threatening							
Punching							
Kicking							
Spitting							
Stabbing							
Hitting (with a weapon)							
Excluding							
Unwanted sexual advances							
Bullying on the internet							
Other							

Session 1, Element 3: How big a deal is my violence?

Using the accompanying handout 'My use of violence', begin this element by exploring the 'good' things and the 'less good' things about the young person's current use of violence and, using open-ended questions and reflective listening skills, explore the young person's thoughts and feelings with regard to the above. Work for 5–10 minutes and then summarize where you are at with the young person.

Aim to get a sense of the how important an issue violence is to the young person and how confident he or she is about doing something about it. A simple way to do this is to use a ruler marked from 0 to 10 and ask the young person:

'How big a problem would you say violence is in your life? On a scale from 0 to 10, where 0 is no problem at all and 10 is a huge problem, where would you say you are?'

A similar approach can then be used to explore his or her confidence in being able to do anything about it.

Another more active option is to stand on a spot in the room and say that this represents the young person as he or she is now in how they are handling their life and how they use violence. Move across the room to a new spot and say that this represents where they would like to get to. Explore the 'gap'.

How big is it? Is there a gap at all? Maybe the young person has no real problem with how he or she is handling things, it's other people that do and there is no gap! Again, explore and reflect back where the young person is at in terms of his or her view of the situation.

It is not too critical to get full acknowledgement. 'Acknowledgement, whilst preferable, is neither a sufficient nor a necessary condition of safety' (Turnell and Edwards 1999, p.140). The motivation for a young person to acknowledge his or her violent behaviour may be to do with avoiding negative consequences, while denial may be due to shame or to avoid humiliation. It is also critical that the aspects of violence in meeting the young person's legitimate goals in life in terms of being respected, happy, doing well at things, friendship, standing up for themselves, etc. are recognized and accepted.

The aim is to help the young person secure these goals and what he or she wants in life but to do so in ways that are socially acceptable and also more personally satisfying to them.

At the end of this session, explain to the young person that the start of each of the remaining sessions will begin with the 'Check in' (see p.37 for a reminder of what this is). Participants can keep copies of the handout 'Checking in' and fill them in for subsequent sessions.

✓

Handout: My use of violence

Good points about my use of violence?   Bad points about my use of violence?

How big a problem is use of violence for me?

| 0 | 1 | 2 | 3 | 4 | 5 | 6 | 7 | 8 | 9 | 10 |

No problem
at all

Huge problem
in my life

Why?

. . . .

. . . .

. . . .

How confident am I that I can use less violence?

| 0 | 1 | 2 | 3 | 4 | 5 | 6 | 7 | 8 | 9 | 10 |

Not confident
at all

Totally
confident

Why?

. . . .

. . . .

. . . .

✓

Handout: Checking in

How big a problem has aggression or violence been in my life since the last session?

| 0 | 1 | 2 | 3 | 4 | 5 | 6 | 7 | 8 | 9 | 10 |

No problem
at all

A really big
problem

Why?

. . . .

. . . .

. . . .

Session 2
The Effects of Violence

The main objectives of the session are that the young person will:

- increase their understanding of what violence is

- increase their understanding of the effects of violence

- increase their motivation and confidence to choose non-violence.

Content	Methods and process
Element 1. Welcome and check-in Welcome, introduction, objectives of the session and check-in.	Affirming and positive. See guidance (pp.35–38).
Element 2. Looking at an example of violence	Describe, or preferably show, a clip of violent behaviour (if possible similar to the type of violence that the young person uses). Use the handout to help the young person explore the violence.

Break

Element 3. The impact on the victim	Explore with the young person the effects on him or her of being subject to violence, the effects of violence on other people and if relevant the effects of past traumatic experiences.
Element 4. Taking care of yourself	A short activity or exercise related to self-care, dealing with stress, relaxation, fun, etc. See Appendix 1 for selection, or can be decided with the young person.

Closure: Thank the young person for his or her participation, stress that the work is done, but as they get ready to leave just in a word or two let you know:

1. how they are feeling

2. one piece of learning that the young person will think about or 'practise' before the next session.

Session 2, Element 2: Looking at an example of violence

Present or show an example of a young person being violent. This will be more powerful if a short example can be presented on video or DVD. (Scenarios may be found on DVDs of films, television serials, national soaps or from YouTube. For example, at 45 minutes into the first episode of *The Wire* there is a scene of gang violence.) The example should explain and/or show the context, build-up and how the violence is manifested. It does not need to show extreme violence, indeed it may be better if it doesn't, but gives a sense of an aggressive outburst. The choice of clip is important as it may be too disturbing or too exciting to be useful.

Explain to the young person that the purpose of this exercise is just to get him or her thinking about different issues involved in an outburst of violence. After listening to or watching the violent scenario, work through the questions on the 'An example of violence' handout. Emphasize that it is not a test, with right or wrong answers, nor is he or she expected to provide detailed, definitive answers at this stage. Stress that any behaviour that is being looked at is never easy to understand fully, and all the more so with violence, and that in trying to get a sense of what is going on, it is helpful to look at much more than just the actions of the person, but also what he or she may be thinking and feeling and how these relate to violent actions.

Point out that over the weeks ahead, the young person will try to do this in relation to his or her own behaviour, particularly when violence is used. Without going into detail now, the challenge ahead will be in all sorts of different ways to work on their own thoughts, feelings and actions as they have just successfully done in the example.

Additional questions may be used to process the example further as suggested below:

- Would there be any difference in the scenario if the parties were of the opposite sex?

- What ideas do you have that may have let the young person deal with the situation in a non-violent way?

- What does the young person need to do to try to move away from using such behaviour?

Handout: An example of violence

What are the *actions* that
you would see as violent?

What is the person who
is being violent *thinking*?

What is the person who
is being violent *feeling*?

Think about the connections between *thoughts, feelings and actions*! How does this help us to understand the violence more fully?

What harm has been caused by the violence?

Session 2, Element 3: The impact on the victim

Begin by asking the young person to think about an occasion he or she was subject to physical violence and abuse. Rather than go into detail about the incident ask them to think more about the impact and how they were affected (see handout 'When someone has been violent to you').

After exploring the effects on the young person from his or her example, move on to to asking the young person to think about the victims of violence in general and what he or she thinks about them.

- How would he or she characterize a victim of violence?

- What are the main effects on victims?

- What would make the effects worse?

- Are the effects short-term or long-lasting and why?

If appropriate, the use of a more experiential activity can be considered for this element in terms of a visit to an injuries or victims unit, or accessing material on DVD, particularly if a connection can be made in some way to the violent behaviour that the young person has been using.

(At this point, it is not necessary explicitly to open up the issue of the young person's own victim(s), although some markers may be put down and the young person can be asked to begin to think about how their victim(s) may have been affected as it will be returned to in a future session.)

This may also be the opportunity to gently open up the issue of whether the young person has experienced other traumatic events or incidents in his or her life. This could range from domestic violence, serious accidents, violence, community conflict, para-militarism, racism, criminal behaviour or sexual abuse. The list is endless.

It is critical to recognize the emotional chaos, disorder and confusion that will accompany serious traumatic events in anyone's life (Gibson 1991). The key is the relationship between the effect on the emotions, particularly anger, and the trauma experienced. Anger has long been identified as being a component of traumatic reactions. 'Anger and trauma have an intriguing relationship' (Novaco and Chemtob 1998, p.167). Studies into domestic violence survivors highlight anger along with fear and pain as the key effects. In particular, there is the difficulty of experiencing so much anger against someone but not being able to express it directly because of the fear of the consequences. What then happens to this anger?

There is an element of risk in opening up this issue with young people, and the limits of the programme in providing a therapeutic response have to be recognized. Nevertheless, particularly, but not only, in relation to the issue of young women's violence, some time may need to be devoted to recognizing the emotional distress and disturbance that remains to be endured and faced by the young person. This needs to be acknowledged, whilst working and striving towards less violent future responses to difficult and conflictual situations.

If relevant, the need for access to more therapeutic services should be considered and supported.

✓

Handout: When someone has been violent to you

Think of an occasion when someone has been violent to you! How did it affect you?

What physical injuries did you receive?
(For example, bruising, cuts, fractures or multiple injuries)

. . . .

. . . .

. . . .

. . . .

. . . .

How did you feel?
(For example, frightened, angry, embarrassed, confused, shocked, humiliated, mixed feelings)

. . . .

. . . .

. . . .

. . . .

. . . .

How did it affect your behaviour afterwards?
(For example, loss of confidence, being uncertain, looking over your shoulder, being on edge, drinking or taking drugs, becoming more violent yourself, and so on)

. . . .

. . . .

. . . .

. . . .

. . . .

Session 3
Exploring the Problem of My Violence

The main objectives of the session are that the young person will:

- increase their understanding of the problem of violence in their life

- increase their understanding of their thinking in relation to violence

- increase their motivation and confidence to choose non-violence.

Content	Methods and process
Element 1. Welcome and check-in Welcome, introduction, objectives of the session and check-in.	Affirming and positive. See guidance (pp.35–38).
Element 2. Boom! – What triggers my violence?	Work through a range of possible triggers for the young person's violent behaviour.

Break

Element 3. Working through an example	Using the JACA model, gently explore with the young person one example of their use of violence.
Element 4. Taking care of yourself	A short activity or exercise related to self-care, dealing with stress, relaxation, fun, etc. See Appendix 1 for selection, or can be decided with the young person.

Closure: Thank the young person for his or her participation; stress that the work is done, but as they get ready to leave just in a word or two let you know:

1. how they are feeling

2. one piece of learning that the young person will think about or 'practise' before the next session.

Session 3, Element 2: Boom! – What triggers my use of violence?

Begin by pointing out that there is always a reason for behaviour. The point of this exercise is to help the young person begin to think about the sorts of reasons that he or she has for their violence: in other words, the things that trigger violence.

The young person can be given a balloon for the exercise. The facilitator can then present a selection of the situations listed on the handout 'What makes your balloon blow up?', and the young person blows into the balloon each time the statement or situation described raises the possibility that he or she would be violent. Keep blowing into the balloon until it bursts. Explore issues around why certain situations present as triggers to violence for the young person as well as around emotions being kept in and then maybe finally exploding!

Any of the 'triggers' can be opened up a bit more in terms of whether it mattered who was making the statement or behaving in the ways described to help the young person get a fuller sense of his or her triggers.

The question of whether or not there is absolutely no alternative to violence in relation to any of the triggers can also be gently explored.

(The balloon exercise is optional and other ways can be used to identify triggers.)

Handout: What makes your balloon blow up?

What triggers you towards being violent?

Blow into the balloon every time you think you would make a violent response.

If someone said any of the following things to you:

You're stupid	You're a druggy	You're a swot
You're thick	You're a weakling	You're a nerd
You're a slag	You're a fruit	You're a bully
You're a bimbo	You're a black bastard	You're a snitch
Your mum's a whore…	You're mental	You're a waster
You're a waste of space	You're skinny	You're a hood
You're gay	You're a pimp	You're a hood-rat
You're a fag	You're ugly	You're a gangster rat

If any of the following happens to you:

Somebody bosses you about and tells you what to do	Someone spreading rumours about you/your boyfriend/girlfriend	Not allowed to go home from the unit
Your girlfriend/boyfriend is two-timing you	Lose money/have no money	Your social worker tells you to tidy up your room
In trouble at school	Someone bullying you	Someone disses you
Told to leave a shop	You feel left out	Someone attacks someone who is a friend
Friends get jumped	Parents fighting/split up	Others?

Session 3, Element 3: Working through an example

It has been proposed that in any episode of violence, the person using the violence makes judgements in four key areas listed below (De Becker 1997). In this element the task is to try to help connect the young person to each of the areas and obtain their views. Using the handout or through drawings, or using the four corners of the room, encourage the young person to think again about the example of violence he or she has already been talking about (can choose another if preferred). The challenge is to try to focus on what he or she was thinking in relation to the following:

- What was their *justification* for the violence? Why did they believe it was OK to be violent at that time? Try to get a sense of the young person's mindset, beliefs, ideas, etc. What were they telling themselves to build up their anger to energize themselves to move towards violence?

- Why did they feel that they had absolutely no *alternative*? Why were there no other ways of getting what they wanted without resorting to violence?

- Again, how did they weigh up what the *consequences* might be? How quickly and unconsciously did they do this? Do they remember thinking this won't go any further, it's not that serious, who's going to know, etc?

- Finally, how much *ability* do they have to be violent? How comfortable are they in actually using violence? Is it something that comes easily to them? It is easier to do something that we have done before and has helped us get our way. Did they have to move towards the victim? How did they decide how much violence to use – a slap, a punch, a kick, a weapon? Remind the young person that decisions are always being made. What is the point beyond which the young person would not go?

Acknowledge and affirm the young person in his or her efforts to process the violent incident and gently challenge them to begin to think about each of the above points in terms of whether they are cast in stone and whether there may be other ways of looking at some of the issues. They are significant pointers that will begin to give a sense of the young person's perspective and view of the place of violence within their life.

Handout: Exploring an example of my use of violence

Why did I think it was OK for me to use violence?

What else could I have done instead of using violence?

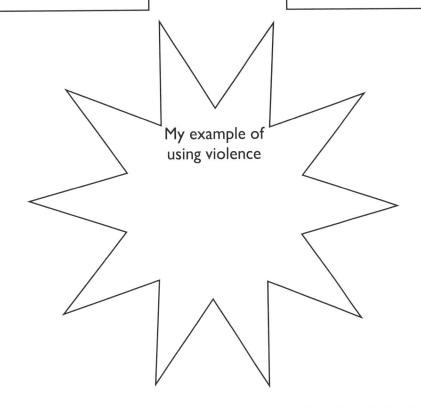

My example of using violence

How did I weigh up the consequences of deciding to use violence?

How comfortable was I with using violence?

Session 4
I'm Not the Problem

The main objectives of the session are that the young person will:

- become more aware of the role of violence in their life

- explore their history of violence

- increase their motivation and confidence to choose non-violence.

Content	Methods and process
Element 1. Welcome and check-in Welcome, introduction, objectives of the session and check-in.	Affirming and positive. See guidance (pp.35–38).
Element 2. The history of violence in my life	Begin the process of trying to help the young person stand back from the problem of his or her violence and to tell their story about it.

Break

Element 3. Violence is the problem!	Explore in depth the problem of violence within the young person's life now.
Element 4. Taking care of yourself	A short activity or exercise related to self-care, dealing with stress, relaxation, fun, etc. See Appendix 1 for a selection, or can be decided with the young person.

Closure: Thank the young person for his or her participation; stress that the work is done, but as they get ready to leave just in a word or two let you know:

1. how they are feeling

2. one piece of learning that the young person will think about or 'practise' before the next session.

Session 4, Element 2: The history of violence in my life

In Elements 2 and 3 of Session 4, the facilitator needs to be directive and purposeful in the use of questioning whilst at the same time empowering the young person to find his or her own voice. The task is to help the young person see his or her violence as something outside themselves that they can relate with and tell their own story about in a way that avoids judgement and shame.

The use of a timeline, either on paper (see handout) or physically on the floor, can help the young person tell the history of the behaviour from before it entered his or her life right up to the present. Some useful questions:

- When did you first become aware of the violence in your life?

- What do you remember before the violence?

- What was the positive intention behind the violence?

- How was it the best choice available to you at that time?

- In what ways was it positive?

- Can you imagine it as a friend, as a person?

- If so, what was it like? – Male or female? – What did it look like? – Can you draw it? – How did it behave? – Can you give it a name? – What music did it like? – Did it provide what a friend should provide?

- When was it at its strongest in influence over you? When were you stronger than it?

- Were you able to trust it?

- In what circumstances would you stop being its friend? (Do not press this too much. Leave the question hanging even if you don't get the answer you want.)

Using the timeline, keep in the past from whenever the behaviour came into the life of the young person. It is also possible to have two perspectives of the young person's story. One can be *in one's story*, that is completely associated with the experience through reliving it. Alternatively the young person may step *out of one's story* and be dissociated from his or her experiences, looking at them from the outside whether in the past or the future – literally to be beside oneself. What are the meanings that begin to emerge around the young person's past association with violence?

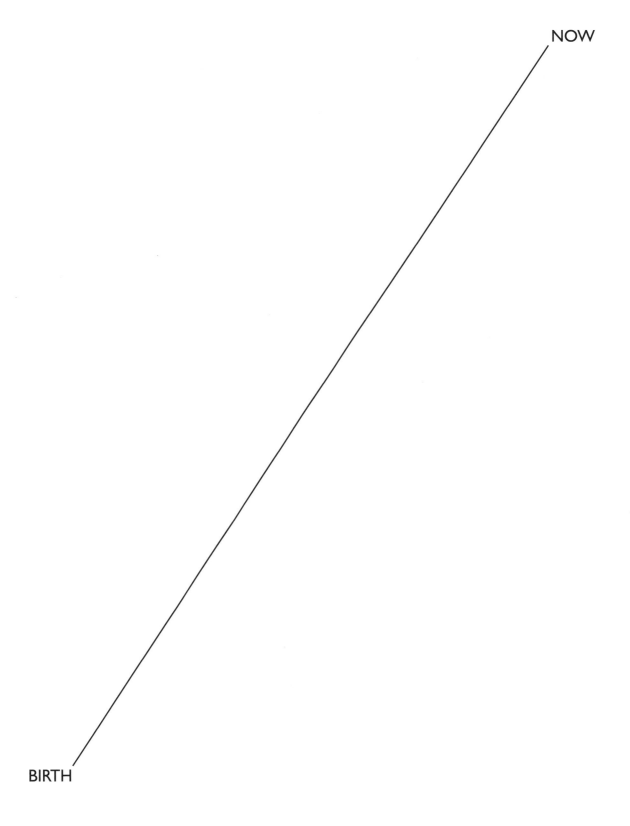

Handout: History of my
relationship with violence

NOW

BIRTH

Session 4, Element 3: Violence is the problem!

In this element the focus is on the violent behaviour as it is operating in the young person's life now. Continue with encouraging the young person to look at the issue of his or her violence from the outside looking in. Possible questions include:

- What does the violence (name it) want you to do with your life? Or to do now? Or in the near future? What are its plans for you? What does it want from you?

- What is it like now? How big a part does it play in your life now or how much control does it have over you (out of ten; ten equalling total control)? Would it have had more or less control over you at some other time? Is it bigger than you or are you bigger than it? Who does the violence want you to become? i.e. What sort of person?

- What does the violence believe in? Value? What rules does it impose on you?

- What are the violence's tricks, tactics, ways of operating, techniques?

- How does it get you to do what you do?

- Compare the behaviour and what it provides to the characteristics of friendship.

- What are its likes and dislikes?

- Who are its allies; who supports it?

- What are its deceits and lies? Were there times when it let you down?

- What way does it speak, its tone, what it says?

The challenge is to engage in a conversation working alongside the young person, not leading but gently hearing the story of the violence in his or her life. The aim is to try to help develop the violent behaviour's separate personality. It is important that an individual personality emerges and is not shaped by the facilitator who should never assume they know how the problem works.

The programme has a strong developmental and historical orientation and will try to help the young person see the continuity between how he or she was dealing with things in the past with the use of violence and their moving (hopefully) to a new position, where their basic goals and what they value remain the same, in terms of autonomy, choice, relationships, happiness, etc. but the ways in which they strive for these will be different.

Session 5
The Effects of My Use of Violence

The main objectives of the session are that the young person will:

- become more aware of the effects of violence on self

- become more aware of the effects of violence on others

- increase their motivation and confidence to choose non-violence.

Content	Methods and process
Element 1. Welcome and check-in Welcome, introduction, objectives of the session and check-in.	Affirming and positive. See guidance (pp.35–38).
Element 2. Achieving my goals Exploring with the young person how the problem of violence has impacted on various aspects of his or her own life	Use the questions outlined in the guidance to get a sense of how the young person feels he or she may have been affected by the presence of violence within their lives.

Break

Element 3. The impact on my victim	Explore the young person's sense of responsibility for his or her violent behaviour, and begin to plan what should be done to address the harm caused.
Element 4. Taking care of yourself	A short activity or exercise related to self-care, dealing with stress, relaxation, fun, etc. See Appendix 1 for a selection, or can be decided with the young person.

Closure: Thank the young person for his or her participation; stress that the work is done, but as they get ready to leave just in a word or two let you know:

1. how they are feeling

2. one piece of learning that the young person will think about or 'practise' before the next session.

Session 5, Element 2: Achieving my goals

Following on from the last session in which the young person has talked about his or her relationship with their violence, the role it has played in their lives, its history and how they see it, the task is now to think about how the problem of violence (or the agreed term that the young person uses for it) is impacting on their life goals.

Once again, the facilitator should help the young person see the violence as something outside themselves that they can talk about objectively. The programme takes the approach that the young person taking part will be no different from other young people in that he or she will be seeking primary human goods, such as a sense of purpose, belonging, relationships, autonomy, etc. Their difficulties with violence have arisen due to a lack of internal skills or because of external conditions that are blocking their access to what they feel is important in their lives.

The approach is about helping them bring to the surface their goals and hopes, not abandoning these, but striving to find ways to acquire them differently. Ultimately it is a 'strengths based approach in that it seeks to equip people with the capabilities to meet their needs, pursue their interests, therefore lead happy, fulfilling lives' (Ward and Maruna 2007, p.109).

The handout 'Overcoming barriers to achieve my goals' may be used to address some or all of the following:

- Take a little time to explore with the young person his or her own goals, life priorities – in other words, their purpose, hopes, dreams and sense of future, their sense of self, their view of themselves as a young man or woman, partner, their self-esteem, their beliefs, values, their abilities, their moods, their relationships, their work, their social life, their physical and mental health.

- Encourage the young person to step back and look at the issue of violence and how it is impacting on what he or she values and wants. The facilitator should accept that the 'violence' may feel threatened by these enquiries and resist or deny or distort responses. Nevertheless, can the young person evaluate the positive or negative effects of violence on what he or she wants? The facilitator may ask why they made such an evaluation. Can the young person begin to see a new story for themselves within which violence has a smaller part?

Handout: Overcoming barriers to achieve my goals

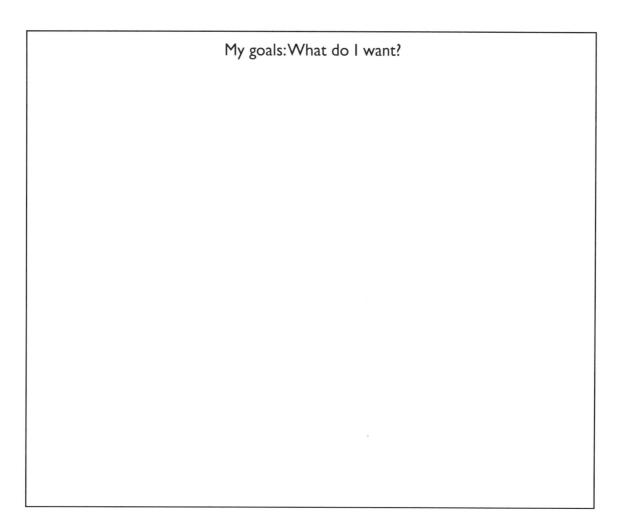

My goals: What do I want?

How is the violence blocking my goals?

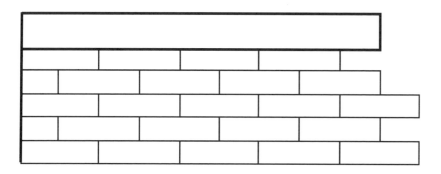

Session 5, Element 3: The impact on my victim

One of the aims of the programme is to help the young person address the harm caused by his or her violence and to show how they intend to choose a more non-violent lifestyle. This element will begin to make more explicit this task.

Explore with the young person how the violence that was used impacted on the person on the receiving end and also begin to identify how the harm done could be made good and what ideas the young person has to this end. Building on the work done in Session 2, and with a reminder of the visit (if relevant) use handout 'The effect of my violence and what I need to do' to open up a range of questions and issues around the effects of the violence on the young person's victim(s).

The aim is to try to increase the young person's awareness and understanding of how the violence has violated and hurt and damaged the victim(s) and what are his or her obligations.

(The work completed in this element will be returned to and built on in the final two sessions of the programme.)

Handout: The effect of my violence and what I need to do

Who has the violence affected?

. . . .

. . . .

What are their needs?

. . . .

. . . .

What needs to be done?

. . . .

. . . .

What are the differences between quick fixes and long-term solutions?

. . . .

. . . .

What can I come up with that might help restore what has been lost, damaged or harmed?

. . . .

. . . .

How much responsibility do I feel I need to take to sort things out?

. . . .

. . . .

Session 6
Gender and Violence

The main objectives of the session are that the young person will:

- become more aware of the relationship between gender and violence

- become more aware of the effects of violence on others

- increase their motivation and confidence to choose non-violence.

Content	Methods and process
Element 1. Welcome and check-in Welcome, introduction, objectives of the session and check-in.	Affirming and positive. See guidance (pp.35–38).
Element 2. Being a young man or woman	Explore with the young person the messages he or she has received about being male or female.

Break

Element 3. Your experiences and expectations	Explore with the young person his or her experiences as a young female or male, their expectations on how they should behave and their attitudes towards violence.
Element 4. Taking care of yourself	A short activity or exercise related to self-care, dealing with stress, relaxation, fun, etc. See Appendix 1 for a selection, or can be decided with the young person.

Closure: Thank the young person for his or her participation; stress that the work is done, but as they get ready to leave just in a word or two let you know:

1. how they are feeling

2. one piece of learning that the young person will think about or 'practise' before the next session.

Session 6, Element 2: Being a young man or woman

Begin by asking the young person if he or she feels that the fact that they are female or male has anything to do with the place that violence has played in their lives.

Ask the young person to begin to think about family members or friends of different gender and whether he or she thinks there are differences between male and female. Acknowledge that there are different view points on this – some people believe that girls and boys have different natures, whilst others believe that basically they are the same but it is the way that society treats them that makes them different.

He or she does not have to accept a particular position; it is more important that they think about how they feel about themselves and the messages they have received about being male or female and how this has influenced the way they behave.

Share the story of the newborn babies in a hospital who were crying and were being watched by adults who did not know whether any infant was a girl or a boy. The experiment found that if the observers thought the child was a girl they tended to regard the distress as fear, whereas if they thought that the child was a boy they were more likely to rate the distress as anger (Fausto-Stirling 1992). Ask the young person to reflect on why this may be...

There are two alternatives for the next stage:

- *Option 1* is to let the young person produce a collage of how he or she sees their own gender. (Please note that significant work is required by the facilitator in preparing for this exercise. It is necessary to have gathered up a large number of magazines, gender-related pictures and images to allow the young person to select from.) Give the individual about ten minutes to produce his or her work. Put the finished work up on a wall, and then just explore, at a general level, some of the different expectations that society places on men and women. 'Every culture has its gender images' (Sammon 1997, p.67).

- *Option 2* is outlined on the handout 'The good and bad of being male or female'. Again the discussion can go further and the young person can be asked to think about all the issues he or she faces, pressures that affect them and expectations they believe are placed on them as a young woman or a young man. Have they their own examples of how they have been treated because of their gender and how their violence helps with this?

Handout: The good and bad of being male or female

Good points about being _____? Bad points about being _____?

3. . . . .

. . . .

4. . . . .

. . . .

5. . . . .

. . . .

6. . . . .

. . . .

7. . . . .

. . . .

How have the above connected to violence?

. . . .

. . . .

. . . .

Session 6, Element 3: Your experiences and expectations

Taking the previous exercise forward encourage the young person to continue to focus on gender issues – using the agree/disagree exercise in handout 'Agreeing and disagreeing about gender and violence' will allow the conversation to go wider. Choose a selection of the Agree/Disagree statements in the handout, as appropriate for the particular young person. Alternatively cards may be made and used with the statements on them and a line of some sort can be used to represent a continuum from strong agreement to strong disagreement and the young person can position themselves on the line at a point to represent their view.

Again it's about gently exploring how the story of his or her violence may be connected to some of the messages they have received. Time can be spent in relation to any of the statements in beginning to help the young person think about the messages he or she has got and the beliefs and ideas that they have come across from within their families, communities and culture as to how they should behave as young women or men.

Gently explore some of the following questions to try to get a sense of their assumptions behind the story of their violence.

- As young men, have they received messages which are about them being hard, macho, not showing feelings, slaggers, dissers, and so on?

- As young women, have they received messages about their lack of worth, their roles as girlfriends, and so on?

- What are some of their beliefs or ideas about their behaviour?

- How did these ideas develop?

- Where did they come from?

- Are they comfortable with these ideas?

- Which ideas are helpful to their goals, which get in the way?

These are externalized constructions, not an integral and unchanging part of the young person's make-up. They are a matter of choice. Conversations can make visible how these beliefs are constructed often to suit others' interests. They enable individuals to achieve distance and awareness and to be amused at how these ideas may have controlled or manipulated them in the past and also take pride in the times that they have challenged them.

The facilitator is not trying to change a young person's thinking or impose their ideas on another. They are being curious and asking questions that they do not know the answer to. The key question is whether a belief is useful or not.

Other issues around how the young person feels he or she is expected to behave because of their race, religion, class, sexuality, or whatever, may also arise and can be explored.

✓

Handout: Agreeing and disagreeing about gender and violence

Agree _____ Disagree

- All young men are violent.
- It's better to fight than to lose face.
- Young women are becoming more violent than before.
- Young men are more violent than young women.
- Violence is exciting.
- It's OK for a young man to hit a young woman.
- It's OK for a young woman to hit a young man.
- It's OK for young men or women to hit each other.
- It's OK to hit your boyfriend/girlfriend if (s)he two-times you.
- Violence is natural.
- There are times when it's OK to hit people.
- It's OK to hit someone with a weapon.
- Violence is just physical.
- You have to fight or you will get walked over.
- If anyone makes a fool of you, you should hit them.
- It's OK to attack other gangs/Protestants/Catholics/Travellers/Black people/ Gays/Chinese/etc.
- You have to fight if you are disrespected.
- If someone tries to get off with your partner you should sort them out.

Session 7
Emotions and Violence

The main objectives of the session are that the young person will:

- become more aware of their emotional life

- become more aware of the relationship between shame and anger and violence

- increase their motivation and confidence to choose non-violence.

Content	Methods and process
Element 1. Welcome and check-in Welcome, introduction, objectives of the session and check-in.	Affirming and positive. See guidance (pp.35–38).
Element 2. Emotions in your life	Help the young person to get a sense of his or her emotional life and also how it may relate to violent actions.

Break

Element 3. Dealing with put-downs and shame	Sensitively open up area of shame and also whether or not past traumatic events are still causing emotional disturbance.
Element 4. Taking care of yourself	A short activity or exercise related to self-care, dealing with stress, relaxation, fun, etc. See Appendix 1 for a selection, or can be decided with the young person.

Closure: Thank the young person for his or her participation; stress that the work is done, but as they get ready to leave just in a word or two let you know:

1. how they are feeling

2. one piece of learning that the young person will think about or 'practise' before the next session.

Session 7, Element 2: Emotions in your life

It is of foundational importance in taking forward this work that young people are helped to 'be able to process and reflect upon powerful feelings rather than simply acting on them' (Jones 2008, p.261).

This is a huge challenge, and the facilitator needs to be realistic about the abilities of young people to manage difficult emotions – a psychologically complex developmental process. Children and young people have fewer mental resources than adults, and specifically in relation to parts of the brain that we like to think of as being rational or reasoning.

Neuroscience tells us that the ability to think reflectively with high levels of awareness through difficult emotional challenges take a good 20 years fully to develop, and key parts of the brain are not completely mature until early adulthood (Goleman 2004). Consequently, the strategies that young people use are based predominantly on emotionality rather than mature logic and reviewing.

There may also be issues of dependency and powerlessness that lead to young people suppressing emotions such as anger and shame. The reality is that developing a toleration of frustration and impulse control requires skills in a consistent and dependable environment and takes time to learn. In addition there is the societal issue referred to by a commentator, reflecting on the American experience and the lack of social capital for many young people, who claimed that children and young people are, on average, 'growing more lonely and depressed, more angry and unruly, more nervous and prone to worry, more impulsive and aggressive' (Goleman 1998, p.11).

Particularly with young men, the issue of shame often proves to be an 'intolerable experience and which their limited ability to process it is quickly converted to rage and violence (Jones 2008).

The facilitator needs to be sensitive to the points made above in exploring the issue of how he or she deals with their emotions with the young person. One starting point may be using the handout 'Identifying feelings and emotions' to consider the many feelings or emotions that they are aware of and write up or visually represent on a flip chart.

Reinforce that emotions are normal, natural human experiences, that every emotion listed will be something that the facilitator and the young person have both experienced at some time in their lives. They are as natural as being thirsty. However, some emotions are clearly more pleasant to experience than others and the challenge in life is for each of us to learn how to deal with coping with difficult emotions. Whilst emotions are in one sense what make us human, and they can tell us useful things about ourselves, we all need to find ways to deal with them and not to bury or repress them.

Ask the young person to return to think about an example of his or her violence. Use the iceberg analogy to ask the young person to identify the feelings they showed in public just before and during the violent incident. Fill these in the part of the iceberg above the water. Then ask the young person to identify feelings that were hidden and below the water line.

The Session 2 handout 'An example of violence' can also be used again to help the young person think further about the emotions which were present before and during the violent incident. Ask the young person how he or she acted out the anger or frustration or shame (actions over which they have some control), rather than how they felt them (emotions over which they have little control). At the same time can they begin to get a sense of the connections between the emotions splashing about inside themselves and their violent actions?

Handout: Identifying feelings and emotions

Joy   Anger   Fear   Sadness

Other emotions

What emotions were splashing about inside you during the violent incident?

Imagine an iceberg. Some of it is above the water and can be seen. Which emotions of yours were seen? Most of the iceberg is below the water.

Which of your emotions were hidden?

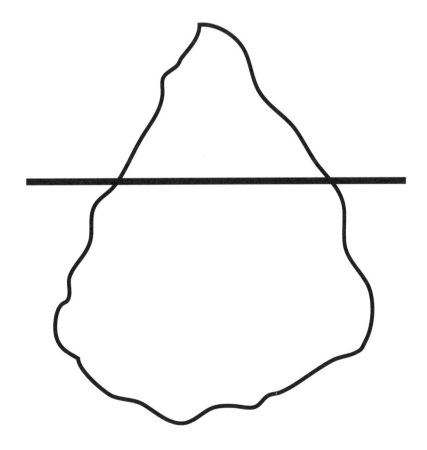

Session 7, Element 3: Dealing with put-downs and shame

Shame is a particularly difficult emotion for any of us to deal with, and more so for adolescents given the ideas on the developmental aspect of emotional intelligence briefly outlined in the previous section. Some young people will not yet have the coping skills to handle situations where they are embarrassed or shamed, so their instinct may be to act out aggressively against those who are shaming them. An aggressive response to shame is a significant predictor of serious violence, and programmes for delinquent adolescents should target emotions and teach them alternatives to aggression in coping with shameful situations (Hart *et al.* 2007).

Some of the literature refers to how often people who are violent, particularly men, feel disrespected. 'The basic psychological motive, or cause of violent behaviour is the wish to ward off or eliminate the fear of shame and humiliation – a feeling that is painful and can even be intolerable' (Jones 2008, p.187). It is always important to be mindful of the connection with masculinity issues around identity and that shame may emerge as a significant factor in understanding violence.

The young person's shame needs to be understood not only in terms of the relations in which it arises, but also in terms of the individual's capacity to process and make sense of it. With a young woman, the shame, despair and degradation of previous abusive experiences may be continuing to play out for them and being vented in outbursts of violence. The handout 'Disrespect, losing face and shame' may be used to open up this difficult area with the young person.

Handout: Disrespect, losing face and shame

What is the most usual way that you experience *shame* or *loss of face* in front of others – or have past experiences left you with such feelings?

....

....

....

....

What happens to you in such situations?

....

....

....

....

How is the use of violence a way of dealing with this?

....

....

....

....

What sorts of ways do you have of dealing with this?

....

....

....

....

Are there any ways you can deal with it that could involve choosing not to be violent?

....

....

....

....

Session 8
Thinking and Decision-Making

The main objectives of the session are that the young person will:

- become more aware of their thinking and how it relates to violence
- make better decisions
- increase their motivation and confidence to choose non-violence.

Content	Methods and process
Element 1. Welcome and check-in Welcome, introduction, objectives of the session and check-in.	Affirming and positive. See guidance (pp.35–38).
Element 2. Thinking about thinking	Using the scenario explore different ways of thinking about the same situation and then explore the young person's thinking within the incident of violence.

Break

Element 3. Making positive decisions	Rehearse with the young person the use of more critical positive thinking in dealing with difficult situations and decisions.
Element 4. Taking care of yourself	A short activity or exercise related to self-care, dealing with stress, relaxation, fun, etc. See Appendix 1 for a selection, or can be decided with the young person (suggest the exercise 'Relaxation and thinking').

Closure: Thank the young person for his or her participation; stress that the work is done, but as they get ready to leave just in a word or two let you know:

1. how they are feeling

2. one piece of learning that the young person will think about or 'practise' before the next session.

Session 8, Element 2: Thinking about thinking

Share the following story with the young person about a group of three young people waiting outside a pub for a taxi and how each of them reacts differently to the same situation. They have been waiting for a while in the cold, and then they see what they assume is their taxi driving up to them and stopping across the street. Suddenly another group of young people appear and run across the street to get into the taxi.

- Young Person 1 starts shouting and screaming over at the other people across the road and runs over to them and starts pulling at the taxi door trying to get in and lashes out at those who have got into the taxi.

- Young Person 2, when he sees what is happening, panics and starts to worry about the trouble they are going to get into and runs off leaving the other two.

- Young Person 3 takes a little while to deal with the situation and tries to calm down Young Person 1 and check with the taxi whether or not it was the one that had been ordered for them.

Ask the young person why each of the young individuals reacted differently, why one reacted aggressively, one reacted passively and the third dealt more positively with the situation. In processing the scenario, bring out the importance of how each young person *thought* about the situation as being significant in how they then felt and reacted. The critical issue is that, confronted with the same event, each young person thought differently about it and as a result had different emotions and feelings and behaved in different ways. Explore with the young person: what were the differences in thinking?

- Young Person 1's thoughts might have been 'That "bastard" ignored us on purpose and picked up those wankers/fuckers/fags, etc. when it should have been us... Who the fuck do those cunts think they are?... I'm always being treated like shit.'

- Young Person 2's thoughts might have been 'Fuck me, there's going to be trouble... Everything always happens to me... I'm better off out of here.'

- Young Person 3's thoughts might have been 'What's going on here? How come they got our taxi? It's stupid starting a big row over this. My friend is going to get into trouble again... What's the best thing to do here?'

In addition or alternatively, the importance of how people think about things can be shown through 'lateral thinking' puzzles such as the nine dots box (see handout 'Thinking about thinking – the nine dots exercise'). The challenge to the young person is to join up all the dots using four straight lines. Once he or she has started drawing their lines they cannot lift their pencil or retrace their line but have to keep going and go through all the dots. Most people tend to think of the nine dots as a box and try to do the puzzle within the outline of the box shape. The breakthrough in thinking that is required for the task is not to feel restrained to keep the lines all in the box – thinking outside the box! (See solution below.

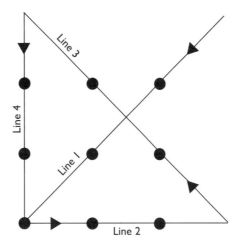

The challenge is to get across to the young person the idea that until one started to think differently about the puzzle and not just see the dots as a box then it was not possible to find a solution. In addition, even by beginning to see the dots as just nine dots and not just a box, it doesn't make the solution easy but it makes it possible. Can the young person see his or her use of violence like this? Until they start thinking about it a bit differently (outside the box) then they will not be able to sort it out. They will need to find new ways of thinking to move away from being drawn into the use of violence.

This conversation can lead on to the issue of *self-awareness* and the ability of everyone to step back to reflect on how they deal with situations – a human gift! If the young person has a pet, the ability of their animal to think in amazing ways could be pointed out. However, whilst both humans and animals can think, the one big difference between them is that humans can think about how they think! Another way to illustrate this is to ask the young person if he or she can, in their own minds, step outside themselves for a moment. Ask them to put their minds up into a corner of the room and imagine that they are looking down and observing themselves as they participate in this session.

He or she should be able to think about how they are thinking in relation to what they are hearing. Can they actually experience themselves thinking? For example, this is interesting and I am agreeing with what is being said; this is rubbish; this is boring; this is challenging me; this is a load of whatever! Maybe they can see that they are not really listening that well because of some other problem or distraction that is going on in their lives at the moment. Can they bring that to awareness and say that they are going to put that on hold until they leave the session and just try to concentrate better on what is going on?

It is this ability that ultimately says that human beings have the chance to make changes to their way of looking at things and to how they will ultimately behave. Affirm that the young person has this gift of self-awareness that allows him or her to work at change. Nobody can control it or take it from them; it is their unique take on their world and what they will choose to do. It is also something that they, like everyone else, have to keep developing throughout their lives.

Handout: Thinking about thinking – the nine dots exercise

Connect the nine dots with four straight lines connected with each other, that is, without your pen leaving the paper.

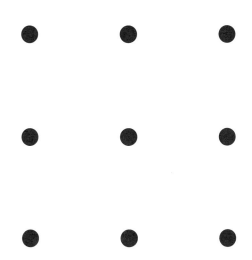

Now think about what you were thinking immediately before your use of violence. Any bad thoughts that didn't help? Were there any other thoughts that if you had brought them into your head, may have led to you not using violence?

New thoughts:

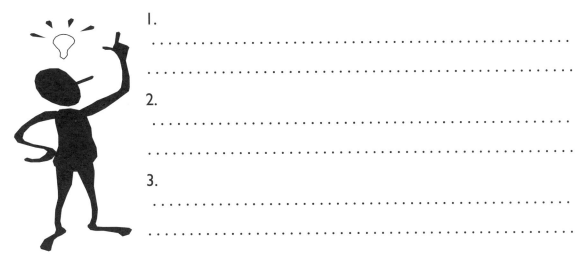

1.
. . . .
. . . .
2.
. . . .
. . . .
3.
. . . .
. . . .

Session 8, Element 3: Making positive decisions

Using the handout 'How would you deal with these situations?' (or cards) work through some of the scenarios that are most relevant to the young person and try to encourage him or her to think about the decisions they would make.

- What are the decisions based on? – Their own views and values?/Their emotions?/Peer pressure and expectations as to how they should behave?

- Can the young person think through the issues and make positive decisions and think about their choices in terms of their future goals and hopes?

- Can they weigh up the possible gains and losses from choices made?

- Can they reflect on the difference between short-term fixes and longer-term consequences?

- How do the decisions impact on their longer-term goals?

As the facilitator, you will need to accept where the young person is at in relation to the issues whilst seeking to help them relate their decisions to their own future goals and aspirations and affirming examples of positive and value-based thinking.

To finish off the exercise it may be possible to make connections to one example of the young person's violent behaviour and whether there were any other decisions they could have taken that may have avoided use of violence.

Handout: How would you deal with these situations?

Can you select and decide how you would deal with some of the following situations? Can you identify the thinking that may help you choose not to use violence?

1. Someone has challenged you to a fight .What do you do? . . . .

. . . .

Why? . . . .

. . . .

. . . .

2. You've been going with a boy/girl for a while and your mates are slagging you about how far you have gone. What do you do? . . . .

. . . .

Why? . . . .

. . . .

. . . .

3. One of your friends is spreading false rumours about you 'cheating' on your partner. What do you do? . . . .

. . . .

Why? . . . .

. . . .

. . . .

4. You are asked to leave the home without permission and stay away overnight. What do you do? . . . .

. . . .

Why? . . . .

. . . .

. . . .

✓

5. Your friend tells you that you would be safer carrying a knife. What do you do?

. . . .

. . . .

Why? . . . .

. . . .

. . . .

6. Someone calls you a… (put in what would most offend you e.g. a fag, bitch, whore, a snitch, etc.). What do you do? . . . .

. . . .

Why? . . . .

. . . .

. . . .

Session 9
Searching for Strengths

The main objectives of the session are that the young person will:

- recognize their positive characteristics and strengths

- identify non-violent choices they have made

- increase their motivation and confidence to choose non-violence.

Content	Methods and process
Element 1. Welcome and check-in Welcome, introduction, objectives of the session and check-in.	Affirming and positive. See guidance (pp.35–38).
Element 2. Choosing a non-violence story	Build the young person's belief in his or her ability to choose non-violent behaviours in difficult circumstances.

Break

Element 3. My positive strengths	Help the young person identify positive attributes and strengths within his or her character and affirm them.
Element 4. Taking care of yourself	A short activity or exercise related to self-care, dealing with stress, relaxation, fun, etc. See Appendix 1 for a selection, or can be decided with the young person.

Closure: Thank the young person for his or her participation; stress that the work is done, but as they get ready to leave just in a word or two let you know:

1. how they are feeling

2. one piece of learning that the young person will think about or 'practise' before the next session.

Session 9, Element 2: Choosing a non-violence story

There will be occasions when the young person has demonstrated that his or her story has not been dominated by violence. This element is about discovering times when the behaviour had little or no influence. The task is to identify an example when the young person chose not to be violent when he or she could have been and then explore this occasion in detail using the handout 'Thinking about your thoughts, feelings and actions' and some of the questions outlined below. (A particularly strong example from a previous check-in could be used.)

First use questions that explore the *landscape of action* – the events, the sequences, time and plot – Who? What? Where? When?

- Where were you when this happened?

- Who were with you? – When did it happen? – How long did it last?

- What happened just before and after? – How did you prepare yourself?

- Was it a decision you made on your own? Have you done this before?

Further questions could then be used to explore the meanings of the events – in terms of the individual's thinking processes, relating these to his or her desires, intentions, preferences, beliefs, hopes, personal qualities, values, strengths, commitments, abilities, plans and purposes. These questions explore the *landscape of identity*:

- What does that say about what you want for and what is important for your life?

- What does that say about your hopes? – What were you intending for your life when you did this? – What does that say about what you were planning?

- What does it say about your beliefs and values? – What values was this action based upon? – What values did this show?

- Can you help me to understand what that says you believe in?

- What rules govern that behaviour?

- What went into doing this? – What did it take to achieve this?

Finally, some questions could explore the *landscape of relationships*:

- How would you describe your relationships at that time?

- What was important for your relationships in your decision to avoid violence?

Handout: Thinking about your thoughts, feelings and actions

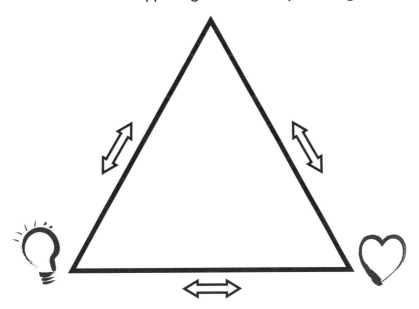

What was happening? What were you doing?

What was your thinking?

How did this fit with what you want from life?

How did this leave you feeling?

. . . .

. . . .

. . . .

Think about the connections between *thoughts, feelings and actions* and how this helped you to choose non-violence on this occasion.

Session 9, Element 3: My positive strengths

Begin the session by genuinely affirming some of the positive characteristics of the young person that have become clear to you as a facilitator up to this point. Take this further and help the young person to pull out some of the strong points in his or her character and to see how these will help them to have a more positive future and achieve some of their goals in life... What are the good things about you? The 'My strengths' handout or cards could be used (laid out on the table/floor).

It is critical to affirm in a genuine way the young person's strengths and life achievements. The more real these can become to the young person, the more they will contribute positively towards the programme goal of moving towards non-violent choices.

Handout: My strengths

Colour at least five that you feel represent strengths that you have.

Other strengths?

What would your best friend say about you?

. . . .

Your mum, dad, gran, some other family member?

. . . .

What strengths would you like to develop?

. . . .

Session 10
Conflict

The main objectives of the session are that the young person will:

- become more aware of how they deal with conflict

- learn about handling conflict less aggressively

- increase their motivation and confidence to choose non-violence.

Content	Methods and process
Element 1. Welcome and check-in Welcome, introduction, objectives of the session and check-in.	Affirming and positive. See guidance (pp.35–38).
Element 2. Responding to conflict	Explore types of conflict that the young person experiences and help him or her get a sense of their 'natural default' positions in dealing with conflict.

Break

Element 3. Is 'win–win' possible?	Explore ways of handling conflict other than winning or losing.
Element 4. Taking care of yourself	A short activity or exercise related to self-care, dealing with stress, relaxation, fun, etc. See Appendix 1 for a selection, or can be decided with the young person.

Closure: Thank the young person for his or her participation, stress that the work is done, but as they get ready to leave just in a word or two let you know:

1. how they are feeling

2. one piece of learning that the young person will think about or 'practise' before the next session.

Session 10, Element 2: Responding to conflict

Begin this element by getting a list of the main conflict situations that the young person experiences that are difficult for him or her. Set them to the side and then encourage the young person to take part in a short active exercise and point out that its purpose will become clear later. In the exercise the facilitator and young person will stand up and face each other across the room without talking and with no physical contact.

The young person is to imagine that the facilitator represents someone or something that they are in conflict with. The young person should try to get a sense that the facilitator represents something that is really annoying and provoking them. The facilitator can then slowly move towards the young person who in their own time should show by movement, posture and stance (still without any speech) how they would normally handle this conflict. Stress again that there is to be no physical contact with the facilitator nor with any object in the room. Give the young person a few moments to act out his or her 'style', and then ask them briefly to describe and explain the position taken. Discuss with the young person using some of the questions below:

- Was the approach direct and threatening, for example, rushing straight up to the facilitator, closing down personal space and 'eye-balling' him or her?

- Was it more tentative and cautious?

- Was it more about turning away and showing more passive or avoidance behaviours?

- How automatic was the response?

- Why was it direct and aggressive or withdrawing and passive?

- What about different types of conflict?

- What role does power have in how potential conflicts would be handled?

Use the 'Handling conflict' handout or demonstrate visually the ideas around the fight or flight responses. These are the normal, almost natural, reactions to conflict. Remind the young person of the reactions to being angered that were in the emotions and shame exercise (Session 7), which are similar when experiencing conflict when the body sometimes short circuits into 'fight or flight'.

✓

Handout: Handling conflict

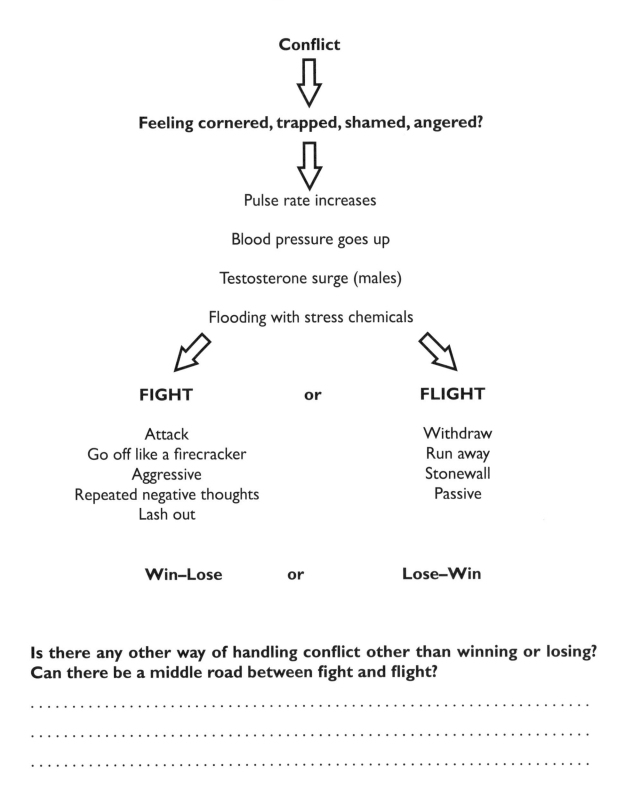

Conflict

⇓

Feeling cornered, trapped, shamed, angered?

⇓

Pulse rate increases

Blood pressure goes up

Testosterone surge (males)

Flooding with stress chemicals

FIGHT   or   **FLIGHT**

Attack	Withdraw
Go off like a firecracker	Run away
Aggressive	Stonewall
Repeated negative thoughts	Passive
Lash out	

Win–Lose   or   **Lose–Win**

Is there any other way of handling conflict other than winning or losing? Can there be a middle road between fight and flight?

. . . .

. . . .

. . . .

Session 10, Element 3: Is 'win–win' possible?

Acknowledge how difficult conflict can be and that in many relationships it can continue for a long time, and even when it may feel as if it's sorted out it can tear people apart again. Explore with the young person examples of when he or she has been on the 'winning' or 'losing' side within a conflict – where they have either got their own way over the other person or have lost to the other person or group. Even if they are on the winning side does it really mean that the conflict has been sorted? Is it likely to break out again? Does it always have to be this way?

Open up the possibility and the idea of a difficult middle way, and rather than conflicts always being win–lose or lose–win, is it possible sometimes for them to be more like win–win? If appropriate this can be illustrated in a light-hearted way with the young person. Ask the young person to agree to take part in a friendly arm wrestling competition. To win a 'prize' each person has to try to put the other person's hand down, and each time they do this they win a prize.

Start the game, and after 'struggling' through a turn or two, ask the young person what way he or she could play the 'game' so that both they and the facilitator could more easily win a lot of prizes. Very quickly it is clear that by taking turns to win and moving their arms back and forward both participants can win. This is the essence of win–win. The big question for the young person is how far he or she can take this idea into ongoing and difficult conflicts with their parents, care workers, social workers, police, neighbours, other young people, gangs or whoever else they may be in conflict with.

Using the handout 'Exploring a conflict I am involved in', try to find a current 'conflict' that the young person is involved in and process it with them by first trying to get the young person to verbalize the other side's position – can he or she, without judging one way or the other, sum up in words as fully as possible what the other side's position is. Encourage the young person as much as possible to stay with this task, acknowledging the strong feelings they may have towards their 'adversary', but ask them in one sense to try to set them to the side for the purposes of the exercise. The ability at least to try to understand fully the other side is critical if there is to be any meaningful sorting out of a conflict. Stress that it is not about agreeing or accepting the 'other' position at this point; it is about taking the time to try to understand it as fully as possible. 'Seek first to understand and then be understood' (Covey 1999).

The second part of the exercise will then involve the young person making his or her position clear. Where do they stand in relation to the conflict and how do they feel they are being treated? The challenge for the young person here is to outline their position using 'I' statements, for example, I feel I am not being listened to; I feel that I am being made to look stupid; I am embarrassed by what has been said or done to me, etc. Can they clearly outline their side without the use of put-downs, insults or abusive statements towards the other side but still fully getting across their position?

Can the young person think about trying the above two steps in the next conflict he or she encounters? First, without going off like a firecracker – can they step back and listen, don't jump in – let the other person have their say – and, if they need more information to understand, try to use questions that are not hostile or judgemental? Only then will they then try to get across their own position as calmly as they can.

How far can this take the young person in seeing a way through the conflict that he or she can live with and does not involve violence or aggression on the one hand or loss of face on the other?

Don't push this too hard. For the young person to master this skill it will take repetition and practice, maybe starting with less serious conflicts. Also, within some families, communities and relationships a conflict may be particularly pernicious and intractable. This reality will have to be recognized and it may be more about helping the young person think about possible strategies to avoid triggering the conflict and not escalating matters.

Handout: Exploring a conflict I am involved in

Step 1: Understanding the other side's position

What does he or she or they want?

If they were sitting across the room from me what would they say?

Without judging or reacting to what the position is – whether I agree or not – can I accurately put it into words and show that I understand?

Step 2: Making myself understood

Now without put-downs, insults against the other side and trying just to use 'I' statements, what is my position in the conflict?

Session 11
Taking Responsibility and Changing

The main objectives of the session are that the young person will:

- prepare for challenges ahead

- identify their goals in relation to future non-violence

- increase their motivation and confidence to choose non-violence.

Content	Methods and process
Element 1. Welcome and check-in Welcome, introduction, objectives of the session and check-in.	Affirming and positive. See guidance (pp.35–38).
Element 2. My ideas about change	Take the young person through ideas about his or her change and where they have got to in choosing non-violence.

Break

Element 3. Dealing with my use of violence Beginning to identify learning, and starting on letter of apology if appropriate.	Use the material to encourage the young person to demonstrate his or her empathy for the victim and begin to think about what they would want to say to them.
Element 4. Taking care of yourself	A short activity or exercise related to self-care, dealing with stress, relaxation, fun, etc. See Appendix 1 for a selection, or can be decided with the young person.

Closure: Thank the young person for his or her participation; stress that the work is done, but as they get ready to leave just in a word or two let you know:

1. how they are feeling

2. one piece of learning that the young person will think about or 'practise' before the next session.

Session 11, Element 2: My ideas about change

Refer back to the young person's goals identified in Session 1 and his or her motivation to try to sort out something about their violence. In this element they will think about the progress they have made in terms of seeing it as a journey. Ask them to think about the flight of an aeroplane. It has just left point A and its destination in its journey is point B. Draw the two points on a flip chart with a line between them, to show the route the plane should take. Point out that during the actual flight wind, rain, turbulence, air traffic, human error and other factors all act on the plane. These move it in different directions so that for most of the time the plane is not on the proper flight course, and in fact it is sometimes going in a different direction.

When people are struggling with change they can be off track just like the plane, and often be going in the wrong direction. Illustrate this on the flip chart with a squiggly line, showing the 'real' route of the plane – up and down, backward and forward, until it eventually reaches its destination. The point is that during a flight a pilot receives constant feedback from radar, ground control, other planes, etc. These tell the pilot that the plane is off track and adjustments can be made to get back on the right path. The absolute crucial fact is that the destination is known so mistakes can be corrected.

Suggest to the young person that this may be a good image for them to have to think about how they are trying to choose non-violence but at times they may slip up or hit difficulties and may go off track. If they do have a slip-up, they will be able to get back on track if they stay clear about the destination. This is their determination to try to move towards non-violent choices, and if that is the way they really want they will have the power to choose to get back on track again.

Explore with the young person where he or she feels they are on the destination of change:

- How far do they really think they have moved from their original position?

- Remember back to the gap in Session 1 – how big was the gap between where they were and where they wanted to get to then and how big is it now?

Affirm the progress that has been made.

Explore with the young person how he or she feels about change. Most people don't like having to change although to get through life all of us have to make changes all the time. Gently explore how they are experiencing the programme and whether it is fitting with their own goals and what they want for their own future. Where is the young person at in relation to each of the following questions?

- To what degree does he or she believe it is possible to make some changes to behaviour?

- What are the important reasons for change?

- How much is his or her behaviour something they decide to use and need to take responsibility for?

- How much more do better internal controls of his or her behaviour need to be developed, or is it sorted?

- How much does he or she need to shift mindset and ways of thinking about violence?

- How much more does he or she need to commit to talking, listening, learning and thinking about these issues?

Reinforce with the young person that change can only come from him or herself – no one can force it on them – it is only if he or she feels that they want to have another story in relation to their violence that the decision to change can be made.

The handout 'Change and choosing non-violence' may be used to facilitate the above conversation with the young person.

Handout: Change and choosing non-violence

Where are you in the journey of change from where you started (A) to choosing non-violence (B)?

A ‾‾‾‾‾‾‾‾‾‾‾‾‾‾‾‾‾‾‾‾‾‾‾‾‾‾‾‾‾‾ B

How ready, willing and able do you feel you are to make a real change in dealing with the use of violence in your life?

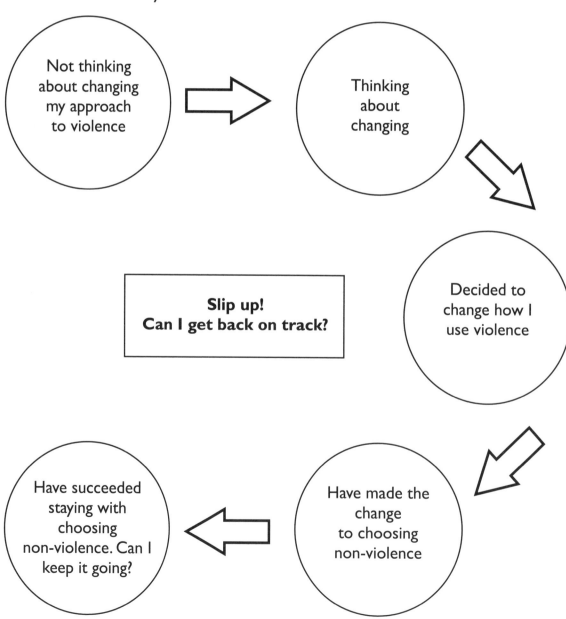

Not thinking about changing my approach to violence

Thinking about changing

Decided to change how I use violence

Slip up! Can I get back on track?

Have made the change to choosing non-violence

Have succeeded staying with choosing non-violence. Can I keep it going?

Session 11, Element 3: Dealing with my use of violence

This element (along with Element 3 in Session 12) will make a start on pulling together what the young person has learned from the programme, and this will be focused on two main areas:

1. his or her increased awareness of the impact and effects of their violence and, hopefully, being able to show a sense of growing empathy for their victim(s), which may be reflected in a letter of apology

2. his or her learning in relation to reducing their future use of violence and committing themselves to non-violence.

The handout 'Dealing with my use of violence' can be used to help the young person begin to think about how he or she would like to respond to their victim. The material can be used flexibly depending on the ability of the young person, but the aim is to assist him or her in beginning to show understanding of what the victim has endured; to focus once more on the experiences of the person(s) at the receiving end of their violence. The emphasis is on trying to get a sense of how much empathy and understanding the young person has gained in terms of the effects of violence on another person.

If appropriate, the young person can be encouraged to write a letter of apology. If he or she does this exercise, it can be followed up in the final session (see handout 'Writing a letter of apology' and Session 12).

✓

Handout: Dealing with my use of violence

What I did

Why am I doing this work?

Sorry?

How was I feeling?

HOW WAS MY VICTIM HARMED?

WHAT HAPPENED TO ME BECAUSE OF USE OF VIOLENCE?

✓

Using some of the ideas on the previous page work through some of the questions below:

What were you doing before you were violent?

. . . .

. . . .

What did you do? (It's always better to tell the truth)

. . . .

. . . .

Why did you do it?

. . . .

. . . .

For example, what happened next? (how was your violence dealt with, who got involved, what have you done about it if anything?)

. . . .

. . . .

What have you learned? (Such as what harm was caused? – think back to what you did in Session 5)

. . . .

. . . .

Would you do it again?

. . . .

. . . .

Are you sorry?

. . . .

. . . .

✓

Handout: Writing a letter of apology

If you wish to write a letter of apology, you can think about it for the next session when you will have time to do it. If you want, you can work on it before the next session.

If you have agreed to write a letter of apology to your victim then well done; this is a really nice way of trying to repair the harm caused by the offence for the victim. It's also a really good way of helping you feel better about yourself.

Remember this is **your** letter so you don't have to follow the ideas below.

Look back at some of the ideas you were thinking about and then put them together in a letter…

As an example, when you start your letter you could say:

Dear…

I am writing this letter to say I am sorry for…

Or you could say

Dear…

I am writing this letter to say what happened…

If you can, try to say how you were feeling at important stages, because this makes the letter sound as if you have thought about what you did a lot more.

As an example:

I am feeling nervous writing about what I did

Carry on trying to say all you can about what you did. This can take a while and it is better to take your time. Try to think how you would feel if you received your letter. If you think you would be upset receiving your letter, and that the person who wrote the letter wasn't really bothered, then chances are the victim will also feel the same receiving your letter.

As you go along read through your work to make sure it makes sense.

Once you have finished your letter you can feel really proud that you have started the process of repairing the harm for the victim, and I bet you're feeling better too.

What happens next?

If you and the facilitator of the Choosing Non-Violence programme agree, your letter may now be passed on to the victim. In some cases they might write back to you, or ask for a message to be passed back to you. The victim does not have to be told any of your personal details, unless you both agree, so any letters or messages will come through whoever is running the programme.

Session 12
Moving On!

The main objectives of the session are that the young person will:

- identify a strategy to deal with a potentially violent situation

- agree the plan to restore the harm done by their violence *or* identify their own plan for the future

- increase their motivation and confidence to choose non-violence.

Content	Methods and process
Element 1. Welcome and check-in Welcome, introduction, objectives of the session and check-in.	Affirming and positive. See guidance (pp.35–38).
Element 2. Can I see it coming?	Identify possible situations in which violence could recur and plan to choose non-violence.

Break

Element 3. Following through to deal with my use of violence	Help the young person summarize his or her learning from the programme and/ or what they would like to say to their victim(s) in relation to what they did and, if appropriate, finish their letter of apology.
Element 4. Ending and reviewing the programme	Celebrate the young person's achievement in completing the programme. End with a bang! (Maruna *et al.* 2003)

Closure: This will be part of the final element in marking the significance of the young person having completed his or her personal programme and journey of learning, and their efforts should be genuinely affirmed.

Session 12, Element 2: Can I see it coming?

Explain that in this element, the young person is going to show how he or she is going to apply the learning they have gained. Begin by identifying a situation in which the young person feels that there would be a real possibility of the problem of violence being present.

- What might happen?

- When?

- Where?

- What mood might I be in?

- What new story could I create that shows my commitment to non-violence?

Other questions can then be developed in trying to enable the young person to create his or her own new story and trying to build up their commitment to their new ways of dealing with it. Some of the open questions below may be used further to reinforce the young person's motivation and sense of efficacy. For example:

- How do your intentions to deal with this difficult situation non-violently connect with your future hopes, your beliefs and values and capabilities?

- How committed are you to this, and is this something new or something you have always stood for and for how long?

- How will this commitment affect your relationships, job, friends, etc?

- What would you call this story?

Session 12, Element 3: Following through to deal with my use of violence

Following up from the previous session, this element will be about continuing to help the young person with a letter of apology (p.124) if he or she has agreed to do one. Alongside this, or as an alternative if a letter is not being completed, the young person can be encouraged to pull together the learning they feel they have gained from the work they have completed.

To meet the restorative requirement of the programme the young person needs to be clear about what he or she has learned from the programme and how they would present this, hopefully along with an apology but certainly with a plan of action to show how they intend to choose a more non-violent lifestyle. The handout 'My new learning' may be used to help go back over some of the themes of the previous sessions and identify any key learning. Alternatively, it may just be about allowing the young person to pick out the key things they feel they have got from the work themselves.

✓

Handout: My new learning

In trying to deal with my past violence I have completed the 12 sessions of the Choosing Non-Violence programme.

1. I am able to take more responsibility in choosing not to be violent by . . . . . .

. . . .

. . . .

2. I deal with my negative nasty feelings by . . . .

. . . .

. . . .

3. I have changed some of my thinking in that I . . . .

. . . .

. . . .

4. I am more aware of the effects of my violence on those on the receiving end, in that . . . .

. . . .

. . . .

5. I see how some of my past experiences and being male (or female) has affected me by . . . .

. . . .

. . . .

6. I handle problems and conflict in a better way by . . . .

. . . .

. . . .

7. My future choices regarding my use of violence are . . . .

. . . .

. . . .

Session 12, Element 4: Ending and reviewing the programme

For this final session, as well as running the usual 'Looking after yourself' elements (see Appendix 2), provide the opportunity for the young person to feedback on the programme and how they have found it (you may arrange for another facilitator to do this – see Appendix 2).

Finally affirm the young person for successfully completing the programme and seek to mark the occasion in some meaningful way.

Encourage the young person to continue to look after him- or herself once the programme has ended.

Appendix I
Exercises for Element 4
'Taking care of yourself'

Emergency relaxation technique

1. Make sure that your body is in an upright position, either sitting or standing.

2. Mentally say 'stop' to yourself.

3. Close your eyes, close your mouth and breathe in deeply through the nostrils. Exhale slowly through the nostrils.

4. Allow your shoulders to drop and the hands to relax. If standing, allow the arms and hands to hang loose. If sitting, allow the arms to bend slightly and the backs of the hand to rest on top of the thighs.

5. Allow the teeth to part slightly, the tongue to rest on the base of the mouth and the jaw to relax.

6. Breathe in deeply through the nostrils. Breathe out slowly through the nostrils. Do at least five inhalations and five exhalations.

7. Allow your breathing to return to normal, allowing it to find its own speed, length, depth and rhythm.

(If necessary, the above exercise could be practised more than once.)

Deep breathing exercise

In either an upright, or preferably, a lying-down position, ask the young person to complete the following breathing exercise as he or she breathes in and out through the nostrils and with the mouth closed (they may choose to close their eyes).

They should place both their hands lightly on the abdomen with the two middle fingers touching in the hollow of the naval. On an inhalation, through the nostrils and with the mouth closed, allow the breath to flow through the nostrils, throat, upper, middle and lower chest and to the abdomen so that the tummy gently rises and the two fingers slightly part.

On the exhalation, allow the breath to flow from the abdomen so that the tummy gently falls and the two middle fingers come towards each other, and the breath passes out through the lower, middle and upper chest, throat and nostrils.

Continue with this practice for a few minutes.

On completion, ask them to take their hands away from the tummy, placing the arms alongside the body.

Ask them to observe their breathing pattern as they breathe normally and note any changes, particularly in their level of stress.

Upon completion of the exercise, thank the young person for participating and ask him or her to think about taking five minutes each day practising this breathing exercise. They need to try to find a time and a place in which they get the peace to do it.

Relaxation and thinking

As a lead-in, point out to the young person that the way they think is also related to their physical condition. If they are very tired or very agitated they will perceive things differently from if they are calm and relaxed and maybe not make as good decisions. This short relaxation exercise is aimed at trying to help them keep their physiological arousal level within reasonable limits day in, day out, so that when something agitating or provoking occurs, their baseline is not so high that they immediately shoot to a dangerously high level.

In this session, the emphasis will be on calm natural breathing but will also introduce a thinking (cognitive) element, which is just about saying a soothing word or phrase to oneself, developing a more passive attitude and learning to relax.

Give the young person a moment or two to make themselves comfortable in their seat or to lie down if they prefer. Appropriate music can be put on and the following script can be used:

> Now you are going to take some time to practise relaxation techniques. In whichever position you have chosen, make sure that you are comfortable. Close your eyes and with the mouth closed take one deep breath in through the nostrils...then, exhale slowly, through the nostrils. Continue

to breathe in and out through the nostrils at your own natural rate for five breaths. Now on each exhalation, mentally repeat the word 'calm' to yourself. Continue this practice for a few breaths. [You can use whatever word you want – cool, chilled, etc.]

The next part of the exercise is to develop a passive attitude. Mentally repeat to yourself 'nothing matters'. Continue to repeat this for five minutes. As thoughts come into your head, try to mentally set them to the side. Try not to judge or analyse the thoughts – let them come in and go out – it doesn't matter what they are. Take note of noises inside and outside the room. Try to let them fade so that there is no particular sound that you are aware of. Stay with this practice. Be aware of your quiet breathing, in and out through the nostrils and the mind becoming passive. Try to feel calmness. Let nothing else matter. Stay with this practice for five minutes.

When the practice is complete, I will tell you that I am going to count from five backwards to one. When I get to one, stretch your arms and legs, yawn and sigh, begin to open your eyes slowly.

Five…four…three…two…one… Bring your awareness back to your position in the room.

Now that you have completed the exercise, know that this is a state that you can go to at any time. Try to make this time available for this practice every day.

Visualization exercise

The young person should get comfortable, sit upright, and be relaxed, not rigid. Allow them a few moments to compose themselves. Tell them that the exercise will last no more than five minutes, during which time they should keep their eyes closed. Ask them to try to stay with the practice to the end of the exercise. The following script may be used:

> Close your eyes. Imagine that you are at the top of a staircase. This staircase will lead you to a place of perfect tranquility – a beautiful garden. [You can use any scene: a beach, a forest, etc.]

> Visualize the staircase before you. See yourself on the top stair. Know that you are about to go down the stairs, one at a time. Mentally, begin to count backwards:

> 10 – You are leaving the day's activity and hassle behind.

9 – Allow sounds around you to fade into the distance so that you are unaware of any sound in particular.

8 – With the mouth closed, become aware of breathing in and out through the nostrils.

7 – Note any tension that you may be holding and then allow your muscles and limbs to become relaxed.

6 – Allow the muscles of the face and head to relax. Allow the teeth to part slightly and the jaw to loosen. Draw the shoulders down.

5 – With each out breath feel that you are breathing out the remains of any tension, worry or anxiety – give it all to the out breath.

4 – As you start to feel calm, be aware of a sense of stillness.

3 – Your breathing is light and your body heavy.

2 – You are at peace as you go down to your special place.

1 – You have arrived at the garden.

Walk to your special seat that has been left for you. Look around you. Take in the scene. Notice the colour, the shapes, the sounds, the smell. Bask in the warmth and comfort of it all. Breathe in the soothing fragrance of the place. Be still…be present…just be…

Rest for a while in this deep inner peace. Give thanks for this place, this still centre. And knowing that you can return to it at any time, choose now to take with you the memory and feeling and experience of its gentle calm. Move slowly towards the staircase. Count your journey back, staying with the scent and bringing its peace and deep relaxation with you as you go back up. 1 2 3 4 5 6 7 8 9…10.

When you reach 10 you are once again back where you started. Rest for a moment on your chair, then, in your own time, wriggle your toes and fingers, open your eyes and gently come back into the present, refreshed and energized. Without rush or hassle, come back into the here and now as we finish the session.

Muscular relaxation

It is best to do the exercise on the floor but it can be practised in a chair. Playing soft, relaxing music in the background can be helpful to this session.

Give a moment or two for the young person to get ready and then take him or her through the following script:

Sit or lie down quietly with the back straight and the arms resting on top of the thighs if sitting or the arms alongside the body with the backs of the hands on the floor. Allow the fingers to curl gently. Allow the body to settle with feet apart. Allow the feet to fall away from each other if lying on the floor.

Keeping the mouth closed, inhale and exhale through the nostrils. Allow the stomach to rise on the inhalation and fall on the exhalation. Concentrate on establishing this slow relaxed breathing pattern for about five minutes.

To relax the muscles:

- Tense the whole of the right foot, release and let go.

- Tense the whole of the right leg, release and let go.

- Tense the whole of the left foot, release and let go.

- Tense the whole of the left leg, release and let go.

- Clench the right fist as tight as you can, release and let go.

- Tense the whole of the right arm, release and let go.

- Clench the left fist as tight as you can, release and let go.

- Tense the whole of the left arm, release and let go.

- Tense the shoulders by bringing them up towards the ears, hold the tension, release and let go, bringing the shoulders well down.

- Tense the head and face by tightening the forehead, closing the eyes tightly and clenching the teeth. Then release and let go all tension out of the face and head and have the teeth slightly apart in the mouth.

- Feel all tension draining from the body. If you are aware of tension in any part of the body, release it and let it go.

Take your awareness back to the breathing and become aware of any changes in the breathing pattern – the length and depth of each breath.

If any thoughts are rising, do not try to stop or judge them; acknowledge them, then let them go. Allow the mind to settle and become quiet.

Allow the body to enjoy this state of relaxation.

Enjoy the stillness of the mind, the calmness of the body.

When the relaxation is completed, stretch the arms up and over the head and the legs and feet away from the body. Yawn, sigh and fully stretch the whole body. Open the eyes slowly. Stand up slowly, and let the arms hang alongside the body.

Stress awareness exercise

Sit or lie in a comfortable position. Close your eyes. Breathe in through the nostrils and out through the nostrils for several rounds of breathing. Allow the breath to slow down naturally and become light.

Concentrate on the *right side* of the body only. Be aware of the right side of the body only.

As each part of the body is mentioned, take your awareness to that part. Without moving the part, acknowledge any tension, release it and let it go.

Starting on the right side of the body, take your attention to the toes of the right foot, top of the foot, sole of the foot, heel, inner ankle, outer ankle, shin, calf, front of the knee, back of the knee, front of the thigh, back of the thigh, groin, hip, side of the waist, side of the chest, front of the shoulder, back of the shoulder, armpit, front of the upper arm, back of the upper arm, inner elbow, outer elbow, front of the lower arm, back of the lower arm, front of the wrist, back of the wrist, back of the hand, fingers lightly curled, palm of the hand. The whole of the right side of the body. Keep your concentration with the right side of the body. Allow it to become heavy, letting any tension go. Keep concentrating on the right side of the body only for a few moments.

Take your awareness to the *left side* of the body. Acknowledge how the right side of the body feels compared to the left side. Concentrate on the left side of the body only. Be aware of the left side of the body only. As each part of the body is mentioned, take your awareness to that part. Without moving the part, acknowledge any tension, release it and let it go.

Take your attention to the toes of the left foot, top of the foot, sole of the foot, heel, inner ankle, outer ankle, shin, calf, front of the knee, back of the knee, front of the thigh, back of the thigh, groin, hip, side of the waist, side of the chest, front of the shoulder, back of the shoulder, armpit, front of the upper arm, back of the upper arm, inner elbow, outer elbow, front of the lower arm, back of the lower arm, front of the wrist, back of the wrist, back of the hand, fingers lightly curled, palm of the hand. The whole of the left side of the body. Keep your concentration with the left side of the body. Allow it to become heavy, letting any tension go. Keep concentrating on the left side of the body only for a few moments.

Now, take your attention to the back of the neck, back of the head, top of the head, the temples, the brow, the bridge of the nose, right side of the nose, left side of the nose, right cheek, left cheek, upper lip, lower lip; allow the teeth to part slightly and the tongue to rest behind the lower teeth, the chin, the throat, front of the chest, abdomen.

Take your attention to the whole body together. Allow the whole body to become heavy and totally relaxed. Stay with this practice for several minutes.

Bring your awareness back to your position in the room. Allow the breath to deepen slightly. Begin to make small movements with the fingers and toes. Take the body to full stretch with the hands behind the head and the legs out straight. Rub the palms of the hands together to create an inner heat. Cup the hands over the eyes and then open the eyes to the heat. Draw the hand lengthwise over the face. Move from your position in your own time.

Relaxation breathing exercise

This practice should be completed in a sitting position, either on the floor or in a chair. It is not suitable for a lying-down position.

1. Make sure that the body is in a steady, upright position.

2. Close your eyes.

3. Rest the back of the right hand on top of the right thigh and the back of the left hand on top of the left thigh and allow the fingers to curl lightly.

4. With the mouth closed, inhale and exhale through the nostrils for five full breaths.

5. With the back of the left hand resting on top of the left thigh, place the index finger of the right hand on the right nostril. Close the nostril.

6. Breathe in and out slowly through the left nostril only for ten breaths.

7. Bring the hand back to the top of the right thigh.

8. Breathe in and out slowly through both nostrils for ten breaths.

9. Place the index finger of the left hand on the left nostril. Close the nostril.

10. Breathe in and out slowly through the right nostril only for ten breaths.

11. Bring the hand back to the top of the left thigh.

12. Breathe in and out slowly through both nostrils for ten breaths.

13. Bring your awareness back to your position in the room and open your eyes slowly.

Appendix 2
Evaluation Forms

Choosing Non-Violence session record

Session No:. . . . . Title . . . .

Objectives:. . . . .

. . . .

Name: . . . . Date:. . . . .

Element 1:	
Element 2:	
Element 3:	
Element 4:	

Participation (including young person's view of the content): . . . .

. . . .

. . . .

. . . .

Action required:. . . . .

. . . .

. . . .

. . . .

Young person's view of the programme

1. What words best describe how you usually felt in the sessions?

anxious	angry	respected
nervous	guilty	listened to
happy	embarrassed	bored
comfortable	relaxed	interested
uncomfortable	depressed	excited
calm	ashamed	awkward

Any other words: . . . .

2. How helpful have you found the programme in being less violent in your life?

6   5   4   3   2   1

very helpful   not helpful at all

3. What bits helped you the most?

. . . .
. . . .
. . . .

4. What bits did not help so much?

. . . .
. . . .
. . . .

5. How much time did you think about not being violent between the sessions?

. . . .
. . . .
. . . .

6. What do you feel are the main changes you have made that have helped you now to choose not to be violent when before you would have chosen to be violent?

. . . .
. . . .
. . . .

References

Andrews, D.A. and Bonta, J. (2003) *The Psychology of Criminal Conduct* (3rd edn). Cincinnati, OH: Anderson.

Baer, J.S. and Peterson, P.S. (2002) 'Motivational Interviewing with Adolescents and Young Adults.' In W.R. Miller and S. Rollnick (eds) *Motivational Interviewing: Preparing People for Change*. New York, NY: Guilford Press.

Banks, S. (2006) *Ethics and Values in Social Work*. Basingstoke: Palgrave Macmillan.

Batchelor, S. (2005) '"Prove me the bam!" Victimisation and agency in the lives of young women who commit violent offences.' *Probation Journal 52*, 4, 358–375.

Batchelor, S. (2010) 'Girls, gangs and violence: Assessing the evidence.' *Probation Journal 56*, 4, 409.

Bath, H. (1999) *Types of Aggression*. Kingston, ACT, Australia: Thomas Wright Institute.

Belknap, J., Dunn, M. and Holsinger, K. (1997) *Moving Toward Juvenile Justice and Youth Serving Systems that Address the Distinct Experiences of the Adolescent Female*. Columbus, OH: Office of Criminal Justice Services.

Blaxter, L., Hughes, C. and Tight, M. (2001) *How to Research*. Buckingham: Open University Press.

Blum, R., Svetaz, M.V. and Ireland, M. (2000) 'Adolescents with learning disabilities: Risk and protective factors associated with emotional well being: Findings from the National Longitudinal Study of Adolescent Health.' *Journal of Adolescent Health 27*, 5, 340–348.

Bonta, J. (2004) 'Effective practice – State of the art (or science).' *Irish Probation Journal 1*, 1, 57–69.

Carr, A. (2005) 'Contributions to the study of violence and trauma: Multi-systemic therapy, exposure therapy, attachment styles and therapy process research.' *Journal of Interpersonal Violence 20*, 426–435.

Catch 22 (2009) *Girls' involvement in violent offending and gang activity. An overview of the evidence*. London: Catch-22.

Chapman, T. (2000) *Time to Grow*. Lyme Regis: Russell House Publishing.

Chapman, T. and Hough, M. (1998) *Evidenced Based Practice: A Guide to Effective Practice*. London: Home Office.

Child Care Northern Ireland (2000) *Managing Aggression in Child Care Settings*. Belfast: Child Care Northern Ireland.

Clark, M. (2005) 'Motivational interviewing for probation staff: Increasing the readiness to change.' *Federal Probation 69*, 2, 1–9.

Covey, S.R. (1999) *The 7 Habits of Highly Effective Families*. London: Simon & Schuster UK Ltd.

De Becker, G. (1997) *The Gift of Fear*. New York, NY: Dell Publishing.

Farrington, D.P. (1998) 'Predictors, Causes, and Correlates of Male Youth Violence.' In M. Tonry and M.H. Moore (eds) *Youth Violence*. Chicago, IL: University of Chicago Press.

Fausto-Stirling, A. (1992) *Myths of Gender: Biological Theories about Women and Men*. New York, NY: Basic Books.

Feilzer, M., Appleton, C., Roberts, C. and Hoyle, C. *The National Evaluation of the Youth Justice Boards Cognitive Behaviour Projects*. Oxford: Oxford University Press.

Frankl, V.E. (2004) *Man's Search for Meaning*. London: Rider.

Freeman, J., Epston, D. and Lobovits, D. (1997) *Playful Approaches to Serious Problems: Narrative Therapy with Children and Their Families*. New York, NY: Norton.

Gibson, M. (1991) *Order from Chaos, Responding to Traumatic Events*. Birmingham: Ventura Press.

Gilligan, J. (2000) *Violence: Reflections on Our Deadliest Epidemic*. London: Jessica Kingsley Publishers.

Goldstein, A.P., Glick, B. and Gibbs, J.C. (2004) *New Perspectives on Aggression Replacement Training: Practice Research and Application.* Chichester: Wiley and Sons.

Goleman, D. (1998) *Working with Emotional Intelligence.* London: Bloomsbury.

Goleman, D. (2004) *Destructive Emotions and How We Can Overcome Them.* London: Bloomsbury.

Hamer, M. (2006) *The Barefoot Helper: Mindfulness and Creativity in Social Work and the Helping Professions.* Lyme Regis: Russell House Publishing.

Hart, J.L., O'Toole, S.K., Price-Sharps, J.L. and Shaffer, T. (2007) 'The risk and protective factors of violent juvenile offending: An examination of gender differences.' *Youth Violence and Juvenile Justice 5,* 367–384.

Heery, G. (2006) *Parents Anger Management Programme.* Cullompton: Willan.

Henry, B., Caspi, A., Moffitt, T.E. and Silva, P.A. (1996) 'Temperamental and familial predictors of violent and non violent criminal convections age 3 – age 18. *Developmental Psychology 32,* 614–623.

Herbert, M. (2000) 'Children in Control: Helping Parents to Restore the Balance.' In J. Canavan, P. Dolan and J. Pinkerton (eds) *Family Support: Direction from Diversity.* London: Jessica Kingsley Publishers.

Iwaniec, D. (2003) 'Identifying and dealing with emotional abuse and neglect.' *Child Care in Practice 9,* 1.

Jones, D.W. (2008) *Understanding Criminal Behaviour: Psychosocial Approaches to Criminality.* Cullompton: Willan.

Jones, K., Cooper, B. and Ferguson, H. (2008) *Best Practice in Social Work: Critical Perspectives.* New York, NY: Palgrave Macmillan.

LeBlanc, M. and Frechette, M. (1989) *Male Criminal Activity from Childhood through Youth.* New York, NY: Springer-Verlag.

Maruna, S., Wright, S., Devlin, R., Brown, J., van Marle, F. and Liddle, M. (2003) *Youth Conferencing as Shame Management: Results of a Long-term Follow-up Study.* Belfast: Youth Conferencing Service.

McVie, S. (2001) *Adolescent Development and Violence: Findings from the Edinburgh Study of Youth Transitions and Crime.* International Association for Research into Juvenile Criminology Conference, Greifswald, Germany.

Miller, W.R. and Rollnick, S. (2002) *Motivational Interviewing: Preparing People for Change.* New York, NY: Guilford Press.

Milner, J. and Myers, S. (2007) *Working with Violence.* Basingstoke: Palgrave Macmillan.

Morrison, G.M. and Cosden, M.A. (1997) 'Risk, resilience, and adjustment of individuals with learning disabilities.' *Learning Disability Quarterly 20,* 43–60.

Newman, T., Mosely, A., Tierney, S. and Ellis, A. (2005) *Evidence Based Social Work: A Guide for the Perplexed.* Lyme Regis: Russell House Publishing.

Novaco, R.W. and Chemtob, C.M. (1998) 'Anger and Trauma: Conceptualisation, Assessment and Treatment.' In V.M. Follette, J.I. Ruzek and F.R. Abueg (eds) *Cognitive Behavioural Therapies for Trauma.* London: Guildford Press.

Pitts, J. (2008) *Reluctant Gangsters: The Changing Face of Youth Crime.* Cullompton: Willan.

Rutter, M., Giller, H. and Hagell, A. (1998) *Antisocial Behaviour by Young People.* Cambridge: Cambridge University Press.

Sammon, S.D. (1997) *Life After Youth: Making Sense of One Man's Journey through the Transition at Mid-Life.* New York, NY: Alba House.

Seymour, K. (2009) '"Real" violence? Gender and (male) violence – an Australian perspective.' *Probation Journal 56,* 1, 29–44.

Stanko, E.A (2002) *Taking Stock: What Do We Know about Interpersonal Violence?* London: Economic and Social Research Council.

Stattin, H. and Magnusson, D. (1989) 'The role of early aggressive behaviour in the frequency, seriousness, and types of later crime.' *Journal of Consulting and Clinical Psychology 57,* 710–718.

Stattin, H. and Magnusson, M. (1996) 'Antisocial development: A holistic approach.' *Development and Psychopathology 8,* 617–645.

Thompson, N. (2003) *Promoting Equality: Challenging Discrimination and Oppression.* London: Palgrave Macmillan.

Thyer, B.A. (1998) 'Promoting Evaluation Research on Social Work Practice.' In J. Cheetham and A.F. Monsoor (eds) *The Working of Social Work*. London: Jessica Kingsley Publishers.

Trotter, C. (1999) *Working with Involuntary Clients: A Guide to Practice*. London: Sage.

Turnell, A. and Edwards, S. (1999) *Signs of Safety. A Solution and Safety Oriented Approach to Child Protection Casework*. London: W.W. Norton.

Ward, T. and Maruna, S. (2007) *Rehabilitation Beyond the Risk Paradigm*. London: Routledge.

World Health Organization (2002) *World Report on Violence and Health: A Summary*. Geneva: WHO.

World Health Organization (2004) *Preventing Violence: A Guide to Implementing the Recommendations of the World Report on Violence and Health*. Geneva: WHO.

Youth Justice Board (2005) *Risk and Protective Factors*. London: Youth Justice Board.